HMH SCIENCE DIMENSIONS™
EARTH'S WATER & ATMOSPHERE

Module E

This Write-In Book belongs to

_____

Teacher/Room

_____

Houghton Mifflin Harcourt™

Consulting Authors

Michael A. DiSpezio

Global Educator
North Falmouth,
Massachusetts

Michael DiSpezio has authored many HMH instructional programs for Science and Mathematics. He has also authored numerous trade books and multimedia programs on various topics and hosted dozens of studio and location broadcasts for various organizations in the United States and worldwide. Most recently, he has been working with educators to provide strategies for implementing the Next Generation Science Standards, particularly the Science and Engineering Practices, Crosscutting Concepts, and the use of Evidence Notebooks. To all his projects, he brings his extensive background in science, his expertise in classroom teaching at the elementary, middle, and high school levels, and his deep experience in producing interactive and engaging instructional materials.

Marjorie Frank

Science Writer and Content-
Area Reading Specialist
Brooklyn, New York

An educator and linguist by training, a writer and poet by nature, Marjorie Frank has authored and designed a generation of instructional materials in all subject areas, including past HMH Science programs. Her other credits include authoring science issues of an award-winning children's magazine, writing game-based digital assessments, developing blended learning materials for young children, and serving as instructional designer and coauthor of pioneering school-to-work software. In addition, she has served on the adjunct faculty of Hunter, Manhattan, and Brooklyn Colleges, teaching courses in science methods, literacy, and writing. For *HMH Science Dimensions™*, she has guided the development of our K–2 strands and our approach to making connections between NGSS and Common Core ELA/literacy standards.

Acknowledgments

Cover credits: (icicles on water tap) ©Arrfoto/Shutterstock; (water drop) ©D. Hurst/Alamy.

Section Header Master Art: (rivers on top of Greenland ice sheet) ©Maria-José Viñas, NASA Earth Science News Team

ISBN   978-0-544-86098-8

9 10   0877   25 24 23 22 21 20 19

4500745873   C D E F G

Michael R. Heithaus, PhD

Dean, College of Arts,
Sciences & Education
Professor, Department of
Biological Sciences
Florida International
University
Miami, Florida

Mike Heithaus joined the FIU Biology Department in 2003 and has served as Director of the Marine Sciences Program and Executive Director of the School of Environment, Arts, and Society, which brings together the natural and social sciences and humanities to develop solutions to today's environmental challenges. He now serves as Dean of the College of Arts, Sciences & Education. His research focuses on predator-prey interactions and the ecological importance of large marine species. He has helped to guide the development of Life Science content in *HMH Science Dimensions™*, with a focus on strategies for teaching challenging content as well as the science and engineering practices of analyzing data and using computational thinking.

Cary I. Sneider, PhD

Associate Research Professor
Portland State University
Portland, Oregon

While studying astrophysics at Harvard, Cary Sneider volunteered to teach in an Upward Bound program and discovered his real calling as a science teacher. After teaching middle and high school science in Maine, California, Costa Rica, and Micronesia, he settled for nearly three decades at Lawrence Hall of Science in Berkeley, California, where he developed skills in curriculum development and teacher education. Over his career, Cary directed more than 20 federal, state, and foundation grant projects and was a writing team leader for the Next Generation Science Standards. He has been instrumental in ensuring *HMH Science Dimensions™* meets the high expectations of the NGSS and provides an effective three-dimensional learning experience for all students.

Program Advisors

Paul D. Asimow, PhD
Eleanor and John R. McMillan Professor of Geology and Geochemistry
California Institute of Technology
Pasadena, California

Joanne Bourgeois
Professor Emerita
Earth & Space Sciences
University of Washington
Seattle, WA

Dr. Eileen Cashman
Professor
Humboldt State University
Arcata, California

Elizabeth A. De Stasio, PhD
Raymond J. Herzog Professor of Science
Lawrence University
Appleton, Wisconsin

Perry Donham, PhD
Lecturer
Boston University
Boston, Massachusetts

Shila Garg, PhD
Emerita Professor of Physics
Former Dean of Faculty & Provost
The College of Wooster
Wooster, Ohio

Tatiana A. Krivosheev, PhD
Professor of Physics
Clayton State University
Morrow, Georgia

Mark B. Moldwin, PhD
Professor of Space Sciences and Engineering
University of Michigan
Ann Arbor, Michigan

Ross H. Nehm
Stony Brook University (SUNY)
Stony Brook, NY

Kelly Y. Neiles, PhD
Assistant Professor of Chemistry
St. Mary's College of Maryland
St. Mary's City, Maryland

John Nielsen-Gammon, PhD
Regents Professor
Department of Atmospheric Sciences
Texas A&M University
College Station, Texas

Dr. Sten Odenwald
Astronomer
NASA Goddard Spaceflight Center
Greenbelt, Maryland

Bruce W. Schafer
Executive Director
Oregon Robotics Tournament & Outreach Program
Beaverton, Oregon

Barry A. Van Deman
President and CEO
Museum of Life and Science
Durham, North Carolina

Kim Withers, PhD
Assistant Professor
Texas A&M University-Corpus Christi
Corpus Christi, Texas

Adam D. Woods, PhD
Professor
California State University, Fullerton
Fullerton, California

Classroom Reviewers

Cynthia Book, PhD
John Barrett Middle School
Carmichael, California

Katherine Carter, MEd
Fremont Unified School District
Fremont, California

Theresa Hollenbeck, MEd
Winston Churchill Middle School
Carmichael, California

Kathryn S. King
Science and AVID Teacher
Norwood Jr. High School
Sacramento, California

Donna Lee
Science/STEM Teacher
Junction Ave. K8
Livermore, California

Rebecca S. Lewis
Science Teacher
North Rockford Middle School
Rockford, Michigan

Bryce McCourt
8th Grade Science Teacher/Middle School Curriculum Chair
Cudahy Middle School
Cudahy, Wisconsin

Sarah Mrozinski
Teacher
St. Sebastian School
Milwaukee, Wisconsin

Raymond Pietersen
Science Program Specialist
Elk Grove Unified School District
Elk Grove, California

You are a scientist!
You are naturally curious.

Have you ever wondered . . .

- why is it difficult to catch a fly?
- how a new island can appear in an ocean?
- how to design a great tree house?
- how a spacecraft can send messages across the solar system?

HMH SCIENCE DIMENSIONS™

will SPARK your curiosity!

AND prepare you for

✓	tomorrow
✓	next year
✓	college or career
✓	life!

Where do you see yourself in 15 years?

Images/Corbis

Collect Data

Observe

Be a scientist.
Work like real scientists work.

Analyze

Be an engineer.
Solve problems like engineers do.

Define Problems

Test Solutions

STEM

Gather Information

Think Critically

Explain your world.
Start by asking questions.

Conduct Investigations

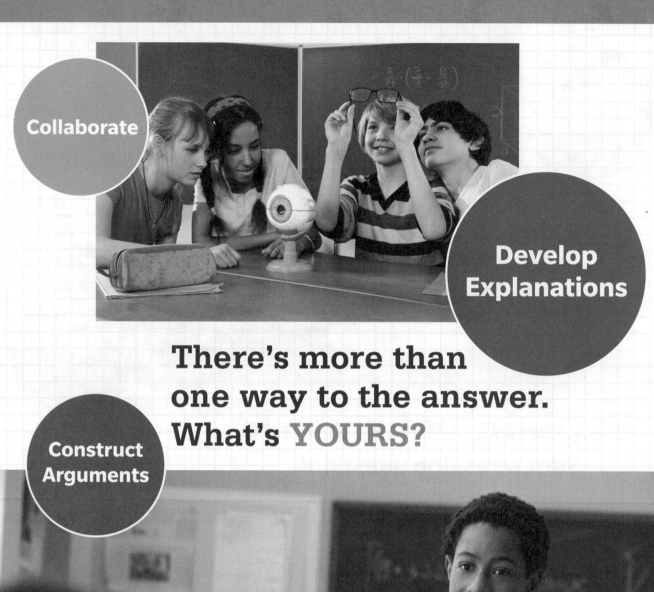

Collaborate

Develop Explanations

Construct Arguments

There's more than one way to the answer. What's YOURS?

YOUR Program

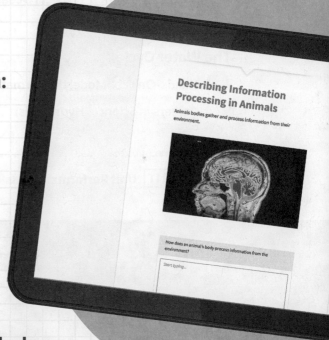

Write-In Book:

- a brand-new and innovative textbook that will guide you through your next generation curriculum, including your hands-on lab program

Interactive Online Student Edition:

- a complete online version of your textbook enriched with videos, interactivities, animations, simulations, and room to enter data, draw, and store your work

More tools are available online to help you practice and learn science, including:

- Hands-On Labs
- Science and Engineering Practices Handbook
- Crosscutting Concepts Handbook
- English Language Arts Handbook
- Math Handbook

UNIT 1

Circulation of Earth's Air and Water

A dark storm approaches a wooden structure built in the water in Maldives.

Weather and Climate

The lush vegetation and abundant water in Erawan National Park in Thailand are the result of a humid tropical climate.

Whether you are in the lab or in the field, you are responsible for your own safety and the safety of others. To fulfill these responsibilities and avoid accidents, be aware of the safety of your classmates as well as your own safety at all times. Take your lab work and fieldwork seriously, and behave appropriately. Elements of safety to keep in mind are shown below and on the following pages.

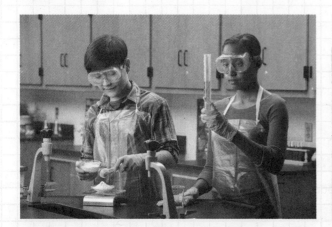

Safety in the Lab

☐ Be sure you understand the materials, your procedure, and the safety rules before you start an investigation in the lab.

☐ Know where to find and how to use fire extinguishers, eyewash stations, shower stations, and emergency power shutoffs.

☐ Use proper safety equipment. Always wear personal protective equipment, such as eye protection and gloves, when setting up labs, during labs, and when cleaning up.

☐ Do not begin until your teacher has told you to start. Follow directions.

☐ Keep the lab neat and uncluttered. Clean up when you are finished. Report all spills to your teacher immediately. Watch for slip/fall and trip/fall hazards.

☐ If you or another student are injured in any way, tell your teacher immediately, even if the injury seems minor.

☐ Do not take any food or drink into the lab. Never take any chemicals out of the lab.

Safety in the Field

☐ Be sure you understand the goal of your fieldwork and the proper way to carry out the investigation before you begin fieldwork.

☐ Use proper safety equipment and personal protective equipment, such as eye protection, that suits the terrain and the weather.

☐ Follow directions, including appropriate safety procedures as provided by your teacher.

☐ Do not approach or touch wild animals. Do not touch plants unless instructed by your teacher to do so. Leave natural areas as you found them.

☐ Stay with your group.

☐ Use proper accident procedures, and let your teacher know about a hazard in the environment or an accident immediately, even if the hazard or accident seems minor.

Safety Symbols

To highlight specific types of precautions, the following symbols are used throughout the lab program. Remember that no matter what safety symbols you see within each lab, all safety rules should be followed at all times.

Dress Code

- Wear safety goggles (or safety glasses as appropriate for the activity) at all times in the lab as directed. If chemicals get into your eye, flush your eyes immediately for a minimum of 15 minutes.
- Do not wear contact lenses in the lab.
- Do not look directly at the sun or any intense light source or laser.
- Wear appropriate protective non-latex gloves as directed.
- Wear an apron or lab coat at all times in the lab as directed.
- Tie back long hair, secure loose clothing, and remove loose jewelry. Remove acrylic nails when working with active flames.
- Do not wear open-toed shoes, sandals, or canvas shoes in the lab.

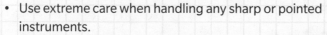

Glassware and Sharp Object Safety

- Do not use chipped or cracked glassware.
- Use heat-resistant glassware for heating or storing hot materials.
- Notify your teacher immediately if a piece of glass breaks.
- Use extreme care when handling any sharp or pointed instruments.
- Do not cut an object while holding the object unsupported in your hands. Place the object on a suitable cutting surface, and always cut in a direction away from your body.

Chemical Safety

- If a chemical gets on your skin, on your clothing, or in your eyes, rinse it immediately for a minimum of 15 minutes (using the shower, faucet, or eyewash station), and alert your teacher.
- Do not clean up spilled chemicals unless your teacher directs you to do so.
- Do not inhale any gas or vapor unless directed to do so by your teacher. If you are instructed to note the odor of a substance, wave the fumes toward your nose with your hand. This is called wafting. Never put your nose close to the source of the odor.
- Handle materials that emit vapors or gases in a well-ventilated area.
- Keep your hands away from your face while you are working on any activity.

Electrical Safety

- Do not use equipment with frayed electrical cords or loose plugs.
- Do not use electrical equipment near water or when clothing or hands are wet.
- Hold the plug housing when you plug in or unplug equipment. Do not pull on the cord.
- Use only GFI-protected electrical receptacles.

Heating and Fire Safety

- Be aware of any source of flames, sparks, or heat (such as flames, heating coils, or hot plates) before working with any flammable substances.
- Know the location of the lab's fire extinguisher and fire-safety blankets.
- Know your school's fire-evacuation routes.
- If your clothing catches on fire, walk to the lab shower to put out the fire. Do not run.
- Never leave a hot plate unattended while it is turned on or while it is cooling.
- Use tongs or appropriately insulated holders when handling heated objects.
- Allow all equipment to cool before storing it.

Plant and Animal Safety

- Do not eat any part of a plant.
- Do not pick any wild plant unless your teacher instructs you to do so.
- Handle animals only as your teacher directs.
- Treat animals carefully and respectfully.
- Wash your hands throughly with soap and water after handling any plant or animal.

Cleanup

- Clean all work surfaces and protective equipment as directed by your teacher.
- Dispose of hazardous materials or sharp objects only as directed by your teacher.
- Wash your hands throughly with soap and water before you leave the lab or after any activity.

Student Safety Quiz

Circle the letter of the BEST answer.

1. Before starting an investigation or lab procedure, you should
   A. try an experiment of your own
   B. open all containers and packages
   C. read all directions and make sure you understand them
   D. handle all the equipment to become familiar with it

2. At the end of any activity you should
   A. wash your hands thoroughly with soap and water before leaving the lab
   B. cover your face with your hands
   C. put on your safety goggles
   D. leave hot plates switched on

3. If you get hurt or injured in any way, you should
   A. tell your teacher immediately
   B. find bandages or a first aid kit
   C. go to your principal's office
   D. get help after you finish the lab

4. If your glassware is chipped or broken, you should
   A. use it only for solid materials
   B. give it to your teacher for recycling or disposal
   C. put it back into the storage cabinet
   D. increase the damage so that it is obvious

5. If you have unused chemicals after finishing a procedure, you should
   A. pour them down a sink or drain
   B. mix them all together in a bucket
   C. put them back into their original containers
   D. dispose of them as directed by your teacher

6. If electrical equipment has a frayed cord, you should
   A. unplug the equipment by pulling the cord
   B. let the cord hang over the side of a counter or table
   C. tell your teacher about the problem immediately
   D. wrap tape around the cord to repair it

7. If you need to determine the odor of a chemical or a solution, you should
   A. use your hand to bring fumes from the container to your nose
   B. bring the container under your nose and inhale deeply
   C. tell your teacher immediately
   D. use odor-sensing equipment

8. When working with materials that might fly into the air and hurt someone's eye, you should wear
   A. goggles
   B. an apron
   C. gloves
   D. a hat

9. Before doing experiments involving a heat source, you should know the location of the
   A. door
   B. window
   C. fire extinguisher
   D. overhead lights

10. If you get chemicals in your eye you should
    A. wash your hands immediately
    B. put the lid back on the chemical container
    C. wait to see if your eye becomes irritated
    D. use the eyewash station right away, for a minimum of 15 minutes

Go online to view the Lab Safety Handbook for additional information.

Circulation of Earth's Air and Water

Kiteboarding requires an athlete to skillfully use Earth's air and water to harness the power of the wind with a large kite.

Most of the time, you probably do not notice the cycling of Earth's air and water. However, sometimes these processes are very noticeable and dramatic. Floods, tornadoes, tsunamis, and even a thunderstorm that wakes you from your sleep are evidence of the power of the cycling of air and water all over Earth. In this unit, you will investigate the processes that cause the circulation of Earth's air and water.

Why It Matters

Here are some questions to consider as you work through the unit. Can you answer any of the questions now? Revisit these questions at the end of the unit to apply what you discover.

Questions	Notes
How does water affect your everyday life?	I think it to survive, I use it for hygene,
How does energy from the sun affect your life?	I get electricity, the earth isn't pitch black
What are some examples of movement of water near where you live?	the shever or lake
Where does the water you drink come from?	the ocean or local fresh water sources
How does the force of gravity on air affect your everyday life?	The gravity afferts water current s and keeps us from floating
How can the movements of air and water make local pollution a global problem?	

Unit Starter: Evaluating Models

In some ways this water fountain is similar to the water cycle on Earth and in other ways it is different. Think about how this fountain might be a useful model for understanding the water cycle.

1. How is the way the water falls in this model similar to the way rain falls on Earth? Select all that apply.

   A. Gravity causes water to fall in both a fountain and rain.

   B. Rain falls both up and down similar to the water in this fountain.

   C. Water is cycled after falling in the fountain and when it rains.

   D. Rain falls in a fixed location like the water in this fountain.

Go online to download the Unit Project Worksheet to help you plan your project.

Unit Project

Energy Flow in the Earth System

Explore the role of energy in the atmosphere and oceans. You will trace how energy from the sun flows through the Earth system as it interacts with air, water, and land.

Circulation in Earth's Atmosphere

Wind blows due to differences in air pressure. These tall grasses on the prairie ripple and sway in the wind.

By the end of this lesson . . .

you will be able to model air circulation in Earth's atmosphere.

Go online to view the digital version of the Hands-On Lab for this lesson and to download additional lab resources.

CAN YOU EXPLAIN IT?

How is it possible for dust from the Sahara to end up in the Amazon?

Sahara

Amazon

Scientists have discovered that about 22,000 tons of phosphorous is deposited in the Amazon every year. The strange thing is that the phosphorus comes from the Sahara! The middle of the Amazon in South America is more than 9,000 kilometers from the middle of the Sahara desert in Africa.

1. What explanation can you suggest for how dust from the Sahara can travel over 9,000 kilometers, across the ocean, and then settle in the Amazon jungle?

Strong winds can push the dust

 EVIDENCE NOTEBOOK As you explore the lesson, gather evidence to help explain how dust and other particles can travel so far.

Modeling Wind and Convection

A hot air balloon floats through the air. The pilot can control the altitude of the balloon by adding or removing heat. But there is no propeller or other system to help it move horizontally. Most hot air balloon rides cover several miles. In 2016, Fedor Konyukhov floated in a hot air balloon all the way around the world in 11 days at speeds of up to 150 miles per hour (241 kilometers per hour)!

2. **Discuss** Think about a hot air balloon traveling around the world in 11 days. How can a balloon travel so far and fast without an engine or other system on board to move the balloon horizontally?

Wind canpush the balloon

Wind

If you go for a walk on a sunny day, it is not uncommon to feel the warmth of the sun and a breeze on your face. Although the sun and the breeze seem to be two separate phenomena, they are actually related to each other. The sun warms both the air and Earth's surface, and the sun warms some parts of Earth more than others. This difference causes pressure differences in the atmosphere and the pressure differences cause wind to blow.

Hands-On Lab
Model the Formation of Wind

You will use a physical model to explain how differences in air pressure form wind.

Air is made of many molecules and particles of matter that are too tiny to see. The motions of air particles cause the particles to run into each other and into objects on Earth. The force of air molecules pressing on other particles and objects is known as air pressure.

MATERIALS
- bottle, plastic, 1 L, with a hole punched in the side toward the bottom
- duct tape
- marshmallows, small
- pump cap that pumps air into a plastic bottle

Procedure and Analysis

STEP 1 Cover the hole in the plastic bottle with a small piece of tape. Fill the bottle $\frac{3}{4}$ full with small marshmallows. Then thread the pump cap onto the top of the bottle and tighten. The pump cap will allow you to put more air into the bottle. Do not pump it yet.

STEP 2 Look at the shape of the marshmallows. Record your observations in the table below.

STEP 3 Squeeze the bottle and observe how it feels. Then shake the bottle and note what you hear. Record your observations.

STEP 4 Hold your thumb over the taped hole while your partner pumps the cap as much as he or she can. This will add more air particles to the bottle. Squeeze the bottle again, and observe the marshmallows. Record your observations.

STEP 5 Carefully shake the bottle, keeping the hole covered. Note what you hear. Record your observations.

Type of Observation	Steps 2-3	Steps 4-5
Shape of marshmallows		
Feel of bottle		
Sound when shaking bottle		

STEP 6 What differences do you observe in the bottle or its contents before air was pumped into the bottle and after?

STEP 7 What do you think will happen if you remove the tape covering the hole?

STEP 8 Before removing the tape, tip the bottle horizontally and shake to distribute the marshmallows evenly over the surface. Remove the tape, and describe what happens.

STEP 9 Explain how the experiment models the formation of wind.

The Formation of Wind

In the activity, you pumped air into a bottle, so the density of air particles in the bottle was greater than the density of air particles outside the bottle. Density refers to the mass per unit volume of a material. Density increases if particles of a material are packed closely. Inside the bottle, the higher density of air particles caused an area of high pressure.

Temperature also affects the density of air particles. When air gets colder, the particles move more slowly and the particles are packed more closely together. As a result, the air becomes more dense. Because cold air is denser and heavier than surrounding air, cold air will sink. When cold air reaches the ground, the air spreads out horizontally. This horizontal movement of air is commonly called *wind*.

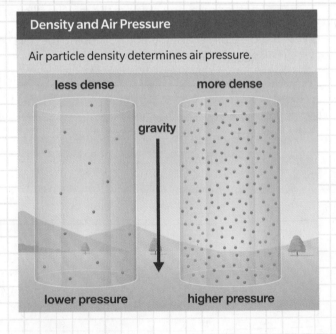

Density and Air Pressure

Air particle density determines air pressure.

less dense   more dense

gravity

lower pressure   higher pressure

3. As air cools, its particles move closer together / farther apart, which increases / decreases its density. Cool air sinks / rises, causing higher / lower air pressure. The cold air spreads out, causing the warm air, which has a higher / lower air pressure, to sink / rise.

Convection

Cool, dense air sinks to Earth's surface and spreads out, causing warm, less dense air to rise. As the warm air moves upward, it eventually cools and becomes more dense than the air around it. This dense air sinks back toward Earth's surface where it begins to warm again. This movement of matter due to different densities is called **convection**.

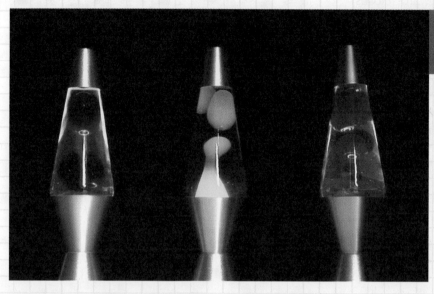

Explore
ONLINE!

These lava lamps show convection. The colored wax at the bottom is warmed, becoming less dense. The more dense material surrounding the warm wax sinks. This pushes the wax up until it cools and becomes more dense than the surrounding material. The dense wax sinks.

4. Which statements about air in the atmosphere are true? For each statement, write T for "true" or F for "false."

___F___ Warm air pushes cool air downward.

___T___ Rising air cools and becomes more dense than the air around it.

___F___ Cool air pushes warm air upward.

___T___ Air that is more dense than the air around it will sink.

5. **Engineer It** Modern houses have systems to control internal air temperatures in times of very cold or hot weather. In these homes, hot or cool air is pumped into the interior of the house to help keep the temperature comfortable. Based on what you know about how cool and warm air circulate in the atmosphere, what might an engineer need to consider when designing a heating/cooling system for a home in a cooler climate? How might the design differ for a house found in a warmer climate?

Convection Cells

Convection can occur on a large or small scale. Look at the air in the diagram. The air near the flame is warm and less dense than the air farther from it. The cool, denser air sinks and pushes the warm air upward. As the warm air moves upward, it loses energy to other air particles. As a result, the warm air becomes cooler and sinks. When the sinking air gets near the flame, it will become warm again. The process continues. This cyclic pattern of movement caused by density differences is called a *convection cell*. Convection cells also form in Earth's atmosphere because the sun heats Earth's surface unevenly.

6. How does the density of air affect its movement in a convection cell?

How Air Moves in a Convection Cell

Warm air above a fire rises as cool air flows in to take its place.

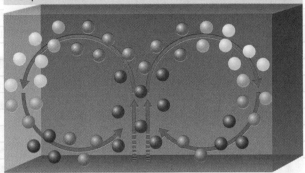

7. Act Together as a group, act out the movement of air near a heat source. Assign roles to classmates, and have each participant explain what is happening to them as they move close to and away from a heat source.

Analyze Winds

Air, land, and water have different properties because they are different materials. One of the ways they are different is that land warms up and cools down more quickly than water does. So when the sun shines on both land and water, the land warms up faster than the water does. The atmosphere changes temperature more rapidly than either land or water. Therefore, the atmosphere is warmed or cooled by being in contact with land or water that is a different temperature.

8. Why does the wind tend to blow from over the water to over the land on a sunny day?

_____

_____

_____

_____

_____

Explaining the Circulation of Air

The Effect of Earth's Rotation

How does wind feel as it blows across your face? Wind is made up of moving particles. Even though you cannot see these particles, they are matter. You also cannot feel or see the movement of Earth. Our planet spins on its axis as it moves through the solar system. This movement has an effect on matter in Earth's atmosphere.

Model the Effects of Earth's Rotation on Matter in the Atmosphere

The photo at the left shows what happens to a drop of ink that is placed at the top of a stationary balloon. The photo at the right shows what happens to a drop of ink that is placed at the top of a rotating balloon. This balloon is being rotated clockwise the entire time that the ink runs down the balloon.

9. **Collaborate** With a partner, develop and use a different physical model to show how Earth's rotation affects matter in the atmosphere. Describe your model. What will you use to represent Earth? How will you model Earth's rotation? What will you use to represent matter in Earth's atmosphere? Before using your model, be sure it is approved by your teacher and you are wearing appropriate safety gear, such as gloves, goggles, and an apron.

10. **Language SmArts** Use evidence from your model to make a claim about how Earth's rotation affects matter in the atmosphere. Describe your evidence and include a diagram or sketch to support your claim.

Wind and the Coriolis Effect

Wind moves from an area of high pressure to an area of low pressure. Winds on a large scale move across Earth because our planet has high- and low-pressure bands. High-pressure bands form near Earth's poles. As the equator gets more solar energy than the poles, low-pressure bands form above the equator. The bands have convection cells between them.

Cool air is denser than warm air is. If no other factors influenced the flow of air in the atmosphere, air at the poles would sink and flow toward the equator, pushing warmer surface air ahead of it. At the equator, the warm air would rise and flow toward the poles, cooling as it moved. Then, the cooled air would sink at the poles. As a result, Earth would have two large convection cells. One would extend from the North Pole to the equator, and the other from the South Pole to the equator. Within these convection cells, air would flow in a straight line as it moves between the poles and the equator.

However, the air in Earth's atmosphere does not move in such a simple pattern. One reason for this is that Earth rotates on its axis.

11. How does the rotation of Earth affect the wind?

Convection Cells

If Earth did not rotate, winds would flow from high-pressure areas at the poles to low-pressure areas at the equator.

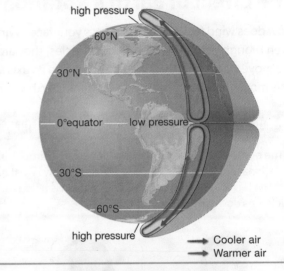

| | Cooler air |
| | Warmer air |

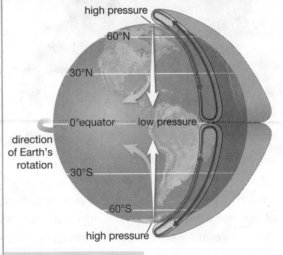

Earth's rotation causes air to deflect, or curve, away from a straight path as it flows across Earth's surface.

	Cooler air
	Warmer air
	Wind direction without Coriolis effect
	Wind as a result of the Coriolis effect

Recall the model of the rotating balloon. The line of ink moving down the balloon was straight when the balloon did not rotate, but when it rotated, the line curved. The spinning of Earth on its axis causes a similar deflection of Earth's winds. This effect of Earth's rotation on the pathway of the wind is called the **Coriolis effect**. As Earth spins, wind in both hemispheres curves.

12. The Coriolis effect affects the direction of the winds in both hemispheres. In which directions do the winds in each hemisphere curve as a result of the Coriolis effect?

Formation of Wind Belts

The Coriolis effect prevents winds from flowing directly from the poles to the equator. The curving horizontal winds combine with vertically moving air to form smaller convection cells that are about 30° of latitude wide. Bands of high pressure and bands of low pressure form between convection cells as shown in the diagram. Cooler, denser air sinks along bands of high pressure. Warmer, less dense air rises along bands of low pressure. This pattern of vertically moving air, curving horizontal winds, and bands of high and low pressure forms three wind belts in each hemisphere.

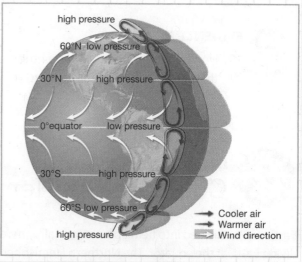

Because of Earth's rotation, winds have curved paths, and Earth has distinct wind and pressure belts.

Global Winds

The sun's rays hit parts of Earth at different angles. Because of this, the sun warms Earth's surface and atmosphere more at the equator than it does at the poles. This unequal heating of Earth's surface and the Coriolis effect cause distinct patterns of global winds. These wind patterns blow in fairly consistent, steady directions across Earth. Each global wind pattern has a specific name.

Model of Global Winds

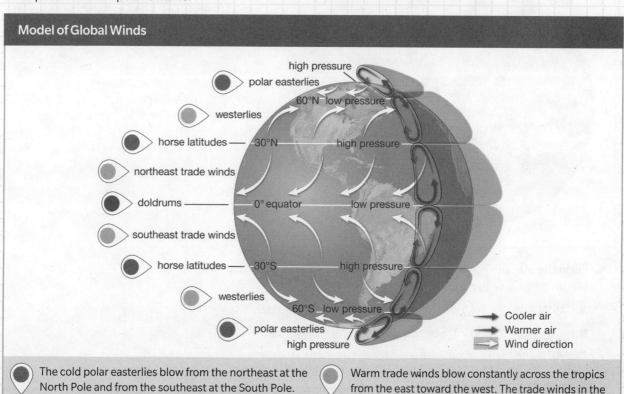

The cold polar easterlies blow from the northeast at the North Pole and from the southeast at the South Pole. They usually form at latitudes greater than 60°.

The westerlies are named for the direction from which they blow—from the west toward the east. They form between 30° and 60° latitude.

The horse latitudes are a narrow zone of warm, dry climates between westerlies and the trade winds. Many deserts are part of the horse latitudes. Horse latitudes are located about 30° north and south of the equator.

Warm trade winds blow constantly across the tropics from the east toward the west. The trade winds in the Northern Hemisphere are called the northeast trade winds, and those in the Southern Hemisphere are called the southeast trade winds. They are located between the equator and 30° latitude.

The doldrums are found where the trade winds of the two hemispheres meet. Winds in the doldrums are very weak, and the weather is consistently calm.

13. How might the global winds contribute to the movement of dust from the Sahara to the Amazon? Record your evidence.

Do the Math
Compare the Hemispheres

Earth can be divided into hemispheres, or half spheres, in different ways. One way is to divide Earth at the equator. The Northern Hemisphere is from the equator to the North Pole, and the Southern Hemisphere is from the equator to the South Pole. Imaginary parallel lines measure north-south distances between the poles and the equator. The equator represents 0°, and the poles represent 90° north for the North Pole and 90° south for the South Pole. The distance between one of the poles and the equator is measured in 1° increments.

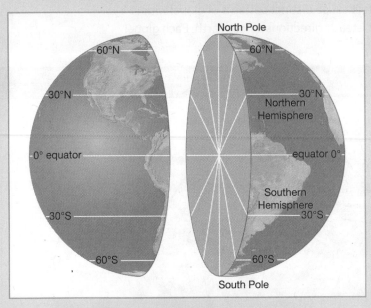

The lines of latitude are named by the angle of a line connecting the latitude and Earth's center and a line connecting the equator and Earth's center. The north or south position of a location is added to the name.

_____

14. Fill in the blank to complete each statement correctly. Remember that *equidistant* means "the same distance."

  A. 45°N and _____°S are equidistant from the equator.

  B. _____°N and 78°S are equidistant from the equator.

  C. 90°N and _____°S are equidistant from the equator.

  D. _____°N and 15°S are equidistant from the equator.

15. The city of Boulder, Colorado, in the United States, is about 40° north of the equator, and the city of San Carlos de Bariloche, in Argentina, is about 40° south of the equator. Which statement is generally true about the wind patterns of these two cities?

  A. Their winds are blowing in opposite directions.

  B. Their winds are blowing from east to west.

  C. Their winds are blowing from west to east.

Relating Air Circulation to the Earth System

What would happen if you were on a sandy beach and a strong wind blew toward you? Do you think some sand might blow on you? Winds can carry many kinds of materials, including sand, as they move across Earth's atmosphere. You can see some of these materials, such as the dust on a playground. Other materials are too small to be seen, such as water vapor molecules. Wind can carry materials thousands of kilometers over oceans and large areas of land.

Moving air also transfers something else you cannot see—energy. When warm air moves over an area where the land or water is cooler, energy is transferred from the warmer air to the cooler water or land. This transfer of energy by wind is an important factor in Earth's weather.

Wind can move large amounts of sediment in a short time.

16. **Discuss** Together with a partner, identify and explain any evidence for the movement of matter and transfer of energy you see in the photo.

The Cycling of Matter in the Atmosphere

Think about sand blowing on the beach. Wind picks up the particles of sand, moves them to a different place, and deposits them. Because of the small size of the sand particles, they can be easily moved by wind. Winds can move many other types of matter, both living and nonliving. Some types are much larger—or smaller—than the sand particles. For example, a slight breeze will move only very light matter, such as a feather, but hurricane winds or tornadoes can move cars, cows, and other large objects. These movements are part of the constant cycling of matter through the Earth system.

17. What factors might determine how far something is carried by wind?

Water

One of the components of air is water—a material needed by every living organism. Water vapor enters the atmosphere from Earth's surface. Then water in the atmosphere is carried by wind from one place to another, often hundreds of kilometers. Water falling from clouds in the form of precipitation is used by living organisms. It also flows across Earth's surface, soaks into the ground, and forms rivers and lakes. Some of this water will enter the atmosphere once again. Water continuously cycles in the Earth system.

Carbon, Nitrogen, and Phosphorus

Other important substances that are cycled in the atmosphere are carbon, nitrogen, and phosphorus. Plants use carbon in the form of carbon dioxide during photosynthesis. You and other organisms release carbon dioxide during cellular respiration. Carbon dioxide enters the atmosphere when fossil fuels burn or when volcanoes erupt. Nitrogen is also released into the atmosphere when fossil fuels burn, during industrial processes, and when bacteria break down organic matter. Plants use nitrogen to make molecules called proteins. Animals use these molecules to build body structures. Living organisms also contain the element phosphorus. As organisms excrete waste or die and decompose, phosphorous is released into soil and water. Water and wind can help cycle phosphorous through the Earth system.

Organic Matter

The atmosphere is also part of the cycling of organic materials and debris. Some living things, such as bacteria, and the remains of once-living organisms can be carried by winds. The same is true for debris, such as ash or other pollutants. Like most of the things carried by wind, you cannot see many of these materials unless they form a dense enough cloud.

EVIDENCE NOTEBOOK

18. How might the cycling of matter in Earth's atmosphere be related to the movement of dust from the Sahara to the Amazon? Record your evidence.

How does wind affect the cycling of matter?

Wind can move clouds hundreds of kilometers.

Wind disperses many plant seeds.

19. **Discuss** Together with a partner, discuss how wind contributes to the flow of matter in Earth's atmosphere. What else does wind move through the atmosphere?

The Flow of Energy in the Atmosphere

Matter is not the only thing that flows through Earth's atmosphere. Energy also flows through Earth's atmosphere and into and out of Earth's subsystems.

The Transfer of Thermal Energy

Thermal energy is the energy we sometimes think of as heat. It is the energy a substance has because of the motion of the particles in the substance. Almost all energy on Earth comes directly or indirectly from the sun. Solar energy travels through space to Earth in a process called *radiation*. Radiation is the transfer of energy by waves such as the light waves from the sun. When the sun's energy is absorbed by Earth's surface, the surface becomes warmer than the air above it. Some particles of air collide with the surface particles, and thermal energy is transferred from the warmer surface particles to the cooler air particles. The transfer that happens when particles touch and transfer energy is called *conduction*. As air particles warm, the particles move farther apart, become less dense, and begin to rise. The flow of air due to differences in density is an example of *convection*. Convection can also be thought of as the transfer of energy due to the movement of matter.

Radiation
Radiation from the sun passes through space and Earth's atmosphere and heats the ground, the water, and structures in the city.

Conduction
Thermal energy can be transferred to and from the atmosphere by conduction when air comes in contact with materials heated by the sun.

Convection
During the day, land heats up quickly and water heats up more slowly. As a result, the air over the water is cooler than the air over land. Convection transfers energy as the cool air flows toward land and causes warm air to rise.

The Transfer of Kinetic Energy

In addition to transfers of thermal energy in the Earth system, there are transfers of kinetic energy. Kinetic energy is the energy of motion. For example, the kinetic energy of wind is transferred to ocean water and powers waves and surface currents. The kinetic energy of the wind also moves material, such as the sand in sand dunes, and changes Earth's surface.

20. How might the transfer of thermal energy and of kinetic energy by wind affect water molecules on Earth's surface and in the atmosphere?

Analyze Atmospheric Interactions

21. For each scenario, identify what parts of the Earth system are interacting, and then describe at least one example of the cycling of matter or the transfer of energy.

A. Clouds forming and then rain falling

Interactions: _____

_____

Cycling of matter: _____

_____

B. A cool breeze making a person shiver

Interactions: _____

_____

Transfer of energy: _____

_____

Continue Your Exploration

Name: _____   Date: _____

Check out the path below or go online to choose one of the other paths shown.

Jet Streams

- **Hands-On Labs** ✋
- **Farming for Energy**
- **Propose Your Own Path**

Go online to choose one of these other paths.

In January, a family from Orlando, Florida, flew by jet to Las Vegas, Nevada, to visit relatives. The trip to Las Vegas took about 4.5 hours, but the return trip to Orlando only took 4 hours. What caused the difference? One possible answer could be the jet streams in the atmosphere.

A jet stream is a narrow belt of fast-moving air that usually forms in the upper atmosphere above global winds. However, some jet streams form as low as 6 km above Earth's surface. Jet streams have wind speeds that are at least 92 kilometers per hour (km/h) and sometimes as high as 322 kph. A jet stream typically flows from west to east.

Jet streams flow along the boundaries between hot and cold air. The greater the temperature difference between the bodies of air, the faster the jet stream will be. Hot and cold air differences are usually greater in the winter, and so jet streams are the strongest during this season. The locations of jet streams can also be affected by the position of the sun during different seasons. For example, in the summer in the Northern Hemisphere, the temperature boundaries are farther north, so the jet stream is farther north. In the winter, the cold air moves farther south, so the jet stream is farther south.

Sometimes the air route from Orlando to Las Vegas crosses the subtropical jet stream. So if the trip to Las Vegas took longer than the trip home to Orlando, then flying west against the jet stream may have slowed down the jet. And when flying from west to east with the jet stream from Las Vegas to Orlando, the wind could be helping the plane move forward.

Jet Streams in the Hemispheres

Both the Northern Hemisphere and the Southern Hemisphere have two main kinds of jet streams. The polar jet stream travels between 50° to 60° north or south of the equator. The subtropical jet stream is closer to the equator.

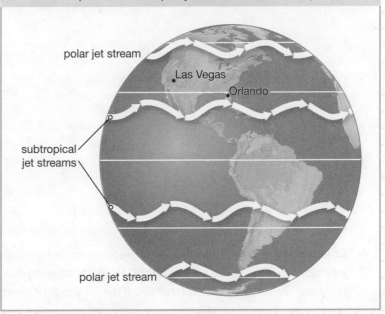

polar jet stream

Las Vegas

Orlando

subtropical jet streams

polar jet stream

Continue Your Exploration

1. What type of technology would be needed to gather evidence of a jet stream?

2. Explain how the sun's heating of Earth's surface and atmosphere may cause the jet streams to move north or south in a given season.

3. Explain why no jet stream exists at the equator.

4. **Collaborate** How would you expect the temperatures north or south of the polar jet stream to differ in each hemisphere? Work together to determine if the air temperature at the surface can tell you if the jet stream is north or south of you.

Can You Explain It?

Name: Date:

How is it possible for dust from the Sahara to end up in the Amazon?

Sahara

Amazon

EVIDENCE NOTEBOOK

Refer to the notes in your Evidence Notebook to help you construct an explanation as to how it is possible for dust from the Sahara to end up in the Amazon.

1. State your claim. Make sure your claim fully explains how material from the Sahara ended up in the Amazon.

2. Summarize the evidence you have gathered to support your claim and explain your reasoning.

Lesson 1 Circulation in Earth's Atmosphere   **21**

Checkpoints

Answer the following questions to check your understanding of the lesson.

Use the illustration to answer Questions 3–5.

3. Which one of the following is a characteristic of all the global winds near the ground?

   A. They all move from areas of high pressure to areas of low pressure.

   B. They all move from areas of low pressure to areas of high pressure.

   C. They all move in the same direction toward the equator.

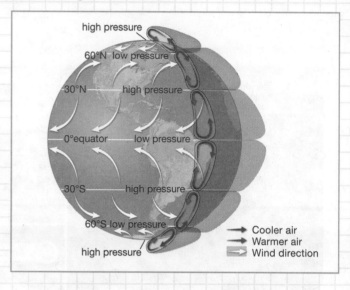

4. Which factors have the greatest impact on the direction of global winds? Choose one.

   A. air speed and the amount of daylight

   B. rotation of Earth and pressure differences

   C. length of the day and temperature of the air

   D. distance from the horse latitudes and size of the sun

5. Many dry desert climates are found around 30° N and 30° S latitude. Which factor has the most influence on the formation of desert climates?

   A. dry air rising at 30° latitudes

   B. dry air descending at 30° latitudes

   C. low amounts of rainfall at other latitudes

   D. high rates of evaporation at the equator

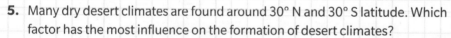

Use the illustration to answer Question 6.

6. As the sun warms Earth's surface and atmosphere, the dark-colored road heats up more than the surrounding fields. Order the statements from 1–4 to describe what happens next.

   _____ The warm air above the road rises and loses energy as it cools.

   _____ The air above the road becomes warmer and less dense than the air above the fields.

   _____ The denser, cooler air over the fields sinks and flows toward the road.

   _____ The denser, cooler air sinks back down to Earth's surface.

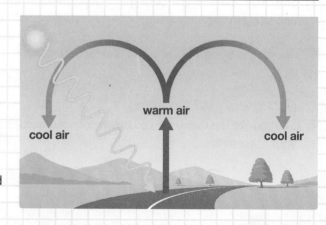

Interactive Review

Complete this section to review the main concepts of the lesson.

Wind forms when air moves from an area of high pressure to an area of low pressure.

A. Draw a convection cell and label the source of heat, the air temperature and density, and the directions of flow.

The unequal heating of Earth's surface by the sun and deflection caused by the Coriolis effect cause distinct patterns of global winds.

B. On a large scale, how do winds move east and west across Earth's surface?

Circulation in Earth's atmosphere moves air around the planet and plays a role in the cycling of matter and the flow of energy in the Earth system.

C. How does wind transfer energy?

Circulation in Earth's Oceans

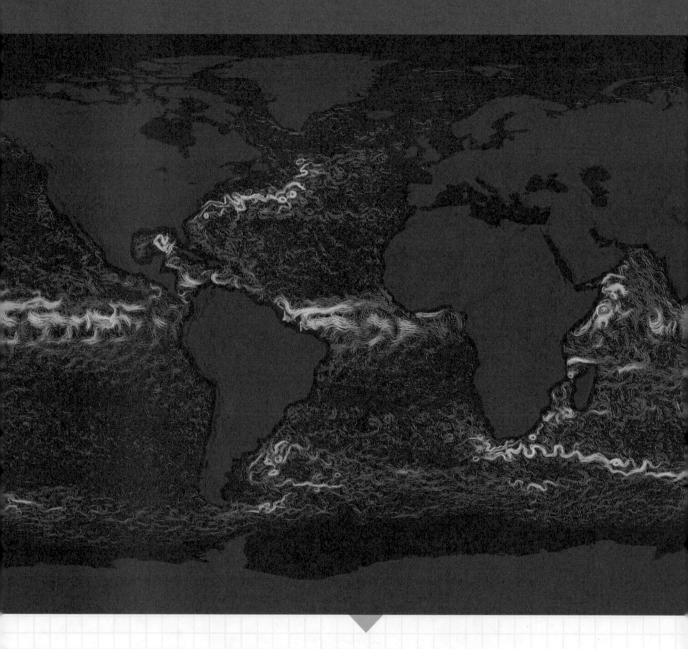

Scientists used satellite data to construct this map of ocean
surface currents. Red and yellow represent faster currents.
Green and blue represent slower currents.

By the end of this lesson . . .

you will be able to use a model of ocean
circulation to explain the flow of energy and the
cycling of matter in Earth's oceans.

Go online to view the digital version of the Hands-On Lab for this lesson and to download additional lab resources.

CAN YOU EXPLAIN IT?

Why does floating garbage tend to build up in certain places in the ocean?

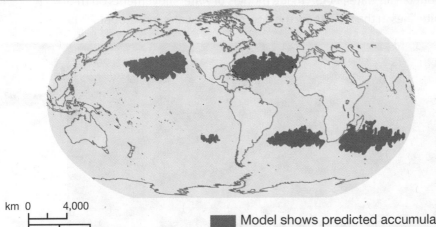

km 0   4,000

mi 0   2,000   4,000

Model shows predicted accumulation of floating garbage 10 years after release

Credit: Adapted from "Origin, dynamics and evolution of ocean garbage patches from observed surface drifters, Figure 1 (c) Tracer accumulation factor after 10 years, doi:10.1088/1748-9326/7/4/044040" from Environmental Research Letters, Volume 7 by Erik van Sebille et. al. Copyright © 2012 IOP Publishing Ltd. CC BY-NC-SA. Adapted and reproduced by permission of Erik van Sebille and IOP Publishing Ltd.

Have you ever wondered what happens when someone throws trash such as a plastic bottle into the ocean? This map shows where floating garbage is likely to collect. The purple areas show where floating garbage is most likely to be found ten years after it is dumped into the ocean.

1. What explanation can you suggest for how floating garbage could be moved around in the ocean?

   By ocean current.

2. What might cause floating objects to collect in one area in a body of water?

   Because the global conve could pusht hem to ther e unjnction

EVIDENCE NOTEBOOK As you explore the lesson, gather evidence to help explain how floating garbage could build up in certain areas of the ocean.

Modeling Surface Currents

Patterns in the Ocean

Using satellite data about ocean water, NASA made models of water movements on the ocean surface. The white lines in the map show the flow of ocean water in October 2005.

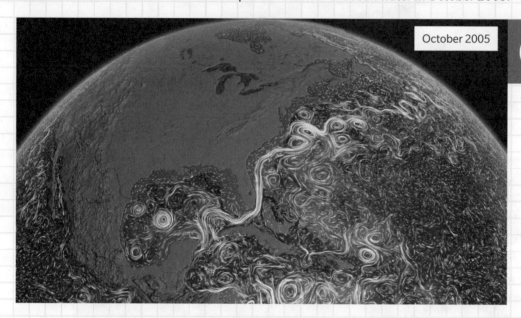

October 2005

▷ Explore ONLINE!

3. What patterns do you see in the movement of the ocean surface?

I see many circles going closn art
wise in the south hand counterin hart

4. Why do you think there is so much movement in the ocean?

Because there are many ocean
currents
Because cerioli's effect

The Formation of Surface Currents

When you look out over the ocean, you might see floating objects being carried along by the movement of water. Although it may be hard to see ocean water moving, it flows in regular patterns. The streamlike movement of ocean water in a regular pattern is called an **ocean current.** As you can see in the map, some ocean currents flow at or near the ocean's surface. This horizontal movement of water in a regular pattern at the ocean's surface is called a *surface current*.

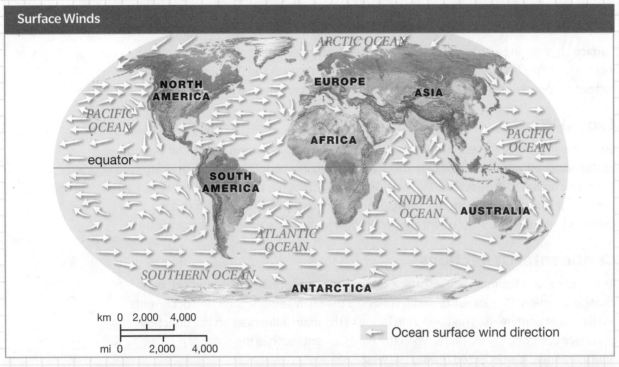

km 0 2,000 4,000

mi 0 2,000 4,000

⬅ Ocean surface wind direction

Surface Currents

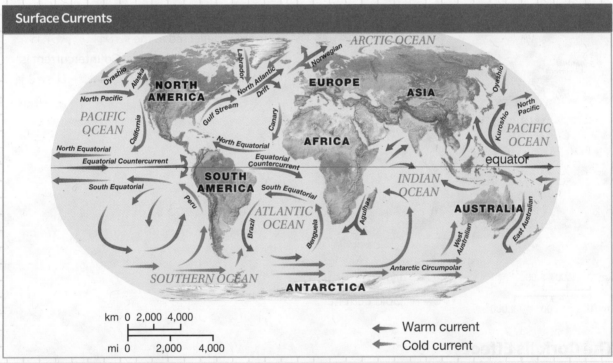

km 0 2,000 4,000

mi 0 2,000 4,000

⬅ Warm current
⬅ Cold current

5. What patterns do you see when comparing the global surface winds with the global surface currents in these maps?

A. In most areas, the winds and the currents move in opposite directions.

B. In most areas, the winds and the currents move in similar directions.

6. Energy from the sun flows into the Earth system. More energy is received near the equator than near the poles. This uneven warming causes _pressure_ differences in the atmosphere. The pressure differences cause _wind_. As wind blows, energy is transferred from the wind to the ocean. The energy transfer causes the water to move in surface ocean _currents_.

WORD BANK
• currents
• pressure
• wind

Factors That Affect Surface Currents

Surface currents in Earth's oceans are influenced by three factors: global winds, the locations of the continents, and Earth's rotation, which causes the Coriolis effect. These factors keep surface currents flowing in distinct patterns around Earth.

Global Winds

Surface winds cause surface currents by transferring energy to ocean water. Think about what happens if you blow across the surface of a liquid in a cup. The transfer of energy from your breath to the liquid causes liquid to move across the cup. In a similar way, winds that blow across the oceans cause ocean water to move. This powers surface currents in the oceans. The currents generally flow in the same direction as the winds.

Continental Deflections

As you can see in the map, when surface currents reach continents, they deflect, or change direction. *Continental deflection* refers to the change in the direction of currents as they meet continents. This deflection is one of the main influences on the direction of surface currents. For example, when the Peru Current reaches the coast of South America, it is deflected toward the west.

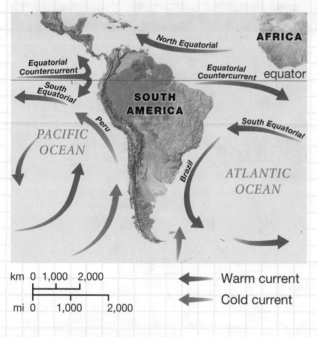

km 0 1,000 2,000

mi 0   1,000   2,000

← Warm current
← Cold current

7. In the Atlantic Ocean, the South Equatorial Current is deflected to the south / north. In the Pacific, the Equatorial Countercurrent is deflected to the east / north and south.

The Coriolis Effect

Earth's surface currents flow in huge circular patterns, called *gyres* (JYRZ). One reason for this circular flow is the rotation of Earth on its axis. Earth's circumference at the equator is larger than its circumference near the poles. So, points near the equator travel faster than points closer to the poles travel. As matter, such as a mass of air, moves from a pole toward the equator, the matter moves more slowly than the ground beneath it does. As a result, winds and water traveling south from the North Pole deflect in a clockwise direction to the right. And winds and water traveling from the South Pole deflect in a counterclockwise direction to the left. This deflection of moving objects from a straight path as a result of Earth's rotation is called the **Coriolis effect.** The Coriolis effect is only noticeable for objects that travel over long distances, such as Earth's wind and water. The Coriolis effect causes water to drift inward a bit toward the center of the gyres.

Surface Currents

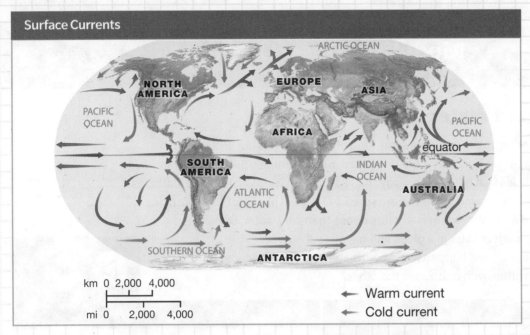

km 0 2,000 4,000

mi 0 2,000 4,000

← Warm current

← Cold current

8. What do you notice on the map about the pattern of the gyres in the Northern Hemisphere as compared to the gyres in the Southern Hemisphere?

EVIDENCE NOTEBOOK

9. Think about how ocean surface currents could affect floating garbage. Record your evidence.

Explain Ocean Temperatures

Scientists use infrared and microwave sensors to gather ocean temperature data. From these data, they make color-enhanced maps that help them study Earth's surface currents.

10. The sea surface temperature at the point labeled *east* is _____. The sea surface temperature at the point labeled *west* is _____.

11. The points *east* and *west* are at the same latitude, so they receive the same amount of solar energy. Explain why points *east* and *west* have different ocean temperatures.

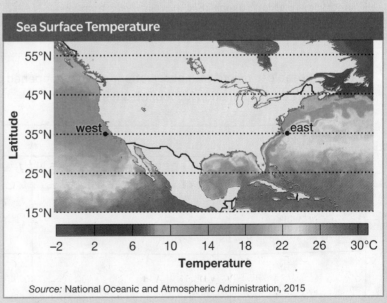

Sea Surface Temperature

-2 2 6 10 14 18 22 26 30°C

Temperature

Source: National Oceanic and Atmospheric Administration, 2015

Modeling Deep Currents

Hot and Cold Water

Hot and cold water are made up of the same kind of particles. But hot and cold water have different properties because of the difference in their temperatures. Cold water has slow-moving particles that have less energy than particles in warm water have. Particles in warm water bounce around more and are spread a little farther apart than particles in cold water are. This makes warm water less dense than cold water. Density is a measure of the amount of mass in a given volume of a substance.

What do you think will happen when cold water and warm water are put in contact with each other, with one above the other?

Explore ONLINE!

Before	After
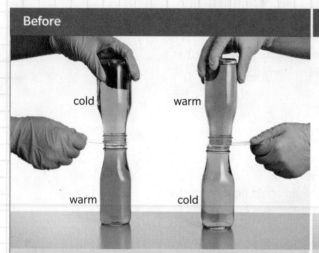	
The blue water is cold. The red water is warm. Bottles of water at different temperatures are placed on top of each other with a plastic card separating the warm water from the cold. The plastic cards are removed from between the bottles. The cold and warm water come into contact.	This shows the same bottles a few minutes after the plastic cards were removed.

12. Use the table to record your observations of what happened in each pair of bottles. Then write an explanation for your observations.

Experiment	Observations	Possible Explanation
Cold above warm		
Warm above cold		

Hands-On Lab
Explore Density Differences in Water

You will design and carry out an investigation to see why sometimes water moves relative to water nearby, and sometimes it does not. You will test water at different temperatures and salinities. *Salinity* is a measure of the amount of salt in water.

   Density is a measure of the amount of mass in a given volume of a substance. It can be measured in the units of kilograms per meter cubed (kg/m^3). Fresh water has a density of about 1000 kg/m^3. Density can be used to predict whether items will float or sink in water. For example, if a piece of metal has a greater density than that of water, the metal will sink in water. In gases and liquids, matter that is more dense than the matter that surrounds it will sink toward Earth's center.

MATERIALS
- container, large
- cups and tablespoons
- ice
- newspaper
- nonmercury thermometer
- permanent pen
- salt
- spoons
- water, warm and cold
- zipper-seal plastic bags, sandwich or smaller (four or more)

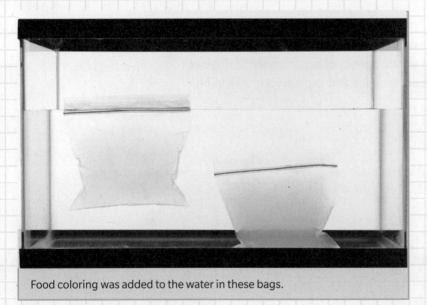

Food coloring was added to the water in these bags.

Procedure and Analysis

STEP 1 Look at the photo. You can test how differences in temperature and salinity affect water's movement by putting your water samples in a zipper bag. Seal the bag so that there are no bubbles left in the bag. It is okay if a little water spills out of the bag as you are sealing it. Then gently place the bag in a large container of water and see where your bag comes to rest.

STEP 2 Write a plan for investigating the relationships of temperature and salinity to the density of water.

STEP 3 On a separate sheet of paper, design a table or other way to collect data from your investigation.

Sample	Water Temperature	Amount of Salt Added	Results

STEP 4 Carry out your investigation and collect data.

STEP 5 What patterns do you see in your results?

STEP 6 Use what you learned in this activity to draw conclusions about the effects of temperature and salinity on the density of ocean water. State your conclusions. Summarize your evidence and explain your reasoning.

STEP 7 How might your conclusions relate to the movement of ocean water?

Density Differences in Ocean Water

Ocean water is not all the same. Differences in the properties of ocean water affect how ocean water moves both horizontally and vertically.

If you have ever accidentally swallowed some ocean water, you would say it is pretty salty. But not all ocean water has the same amount of dissolved salt. One measurement of salinity is the number of grams of salt dissolved in one liter of water, or g/L. The average salinity of all the oceans is about 35 g/L, but ocean water has a range of salinities.

The temperature of ocean water varies as well. For example, in polar regions, water temperature at the ocean surface can be as cold as −1.9 °C. Near the equator, the temperature of surface ocean water can be as high as 30 °C.

Do the Math
Analyze Water Density Data

Analyzing data in graphs can help you see patterns and discover relationships between variables. In each of the graphs below, one variable is held constant so that you can investigate the relationship between two other variables.

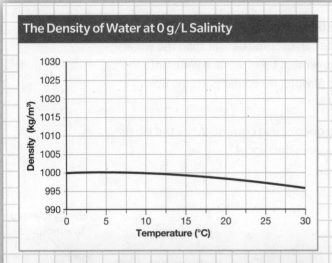

The Density of Water at 0 g/L Salinity

13. This graph shows how the density of water that has no salt dissolved in it changes with changes in temperature.

Water at a temperature of 10 °C has a density of about _____.

Water at a temperature of 25 °C has a higher / lower density than water at 10 °C does.

As the temperature increases, the density of water decreases / increases.

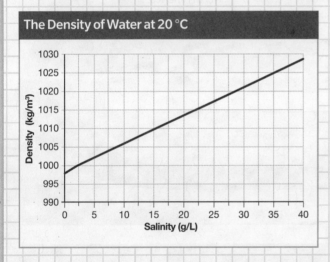

The Density of Water at 20 °C

14. This graph shows how the density of water at a temperature of 20 °C changes with changes in salinity.

Water with a salinity of 20 g/L has a density of _____.

Water with a salinity of 34 g/L has a higher / lower density than water with a salinity of 20 g/L does.

As the salinity increases, the density of water decreases / increases.

Temperature and salinity both affect the density of ocean water. As water gets colder, it becomes denser. An increase in salinity will also make water denser.

The temperature of ocean water changes when the water absorbs or releases energy. For example, solar energy can warm ocean water. And ocean water becomes warmer or cooler when it exchanges energy with the atmosphere.

The salinity of ocean water can be changed by precipitation, by evaporation, by the addition of fresh water, and by the formation of ice in ocean water. When rain falls into the ocean, fresh water is added to the ocean water. So, salinity decreases after a rain. During evaporation, liquid water changes to water vapor that enters the air, but dissolved particles, such as salts, remain behind. So, salinity increases after evaporation. When ocean water freezes, dissolved particles are also left in the liquid part of the water and salinity increases.

15. When rivers flow into the ocean, the salinity of the ocean water
~~increases~~ / decreases because the river adds salt / ~~fresh~~ water.

In an area of the ocean with a lot of evaporation but with little precipitation, the
salinity of the water is likely to increase / ~~decrease~~, and so the density is
likely to increase / ~~decrease~~.

The Formation of Deep Currents

The density of ocean water will increase if the water becomes colder or if the salinity
increases. If this happens, ocean water at the surface can become denser than the water
below it. The denser water sinks. This downward movement takes surface water into the
deep ocean. *Deep ocean currents* are the movement of water in regular patterns below
the surface of the ocean.

16. The diagram shows the circulation of water in a deep ocean current. Write the labels
below in the proper places on the diagram to explain the model.

• a surface current flows toward the pole
• water sinks and forms a deep current

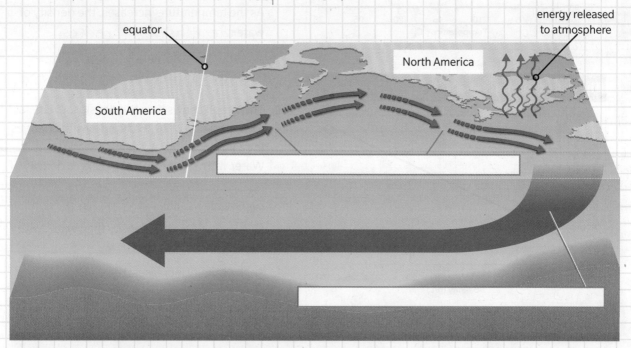

Factors that Affect Deep Currents

Deep currents are driven by density differences in ocean water and by gravity. At Earth's
poles, surface water cools and becomes denser. The denser water is pulled towards the
ocean floor by gravity more strongly than less dense water is and sinks. The cold, dense
water moves in the deep ocean toward the equator, forming a deep current.

Deep currents flow along the ocean floor or along the top of another layer of
water. As a result, several layers of deep currents can occur at any place in the ocean.
Continents and the bottom topography of the ocean affect the path of deep ocean
currents because deep currents are deflected whenever they flow toward land. And the
Coriolis effect causes deep ocean currents to be deflected in the same way that surface
currents are deflected.

17. Engineer It A water heater is a tank in which cold water is heated. Cold water flows into the tank to keep it full. A heating element warms the water inside the tank. The heated water can then be sent to hot water faucets in a building. Assume that a water heater design requires the hottest water possible to be sent to hot water faucets in a building. Where would be the best place for the hot water outlet pipe to be attached to the tank: the top, the middle, or the bottom of the tank? Explain your answer.

Analyze Currents in the Mediterranean Sea

Long ago, people observed water flowing into the Mediterranean Sea from the surface of the Atlantic Ocean and the Black Sea, and from rivers. And they noticed something very puzzling. No matter how much water flowed into the Mediterranean, its sea level remained the same. Some evaporation was occurring, but it was not enough to remove the amount of water that was entering the Mediterranean Sea.

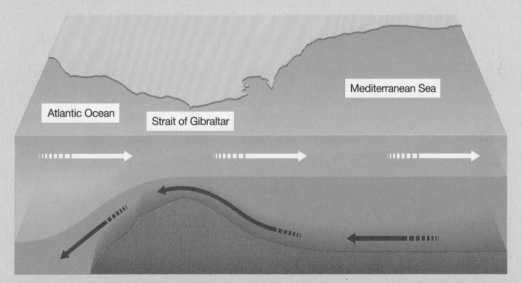

18. What processes in the Mediterranean Sea might explain why the water level of the Mediterranean did not increase, even though all the surface currents were flowing into that sea? The map and diagram may help you develop your explanation.

_____

_____

_____

_____

Relating Ocean Circulation to the Flow of Matter and Energy

Earth's Oceans as a System

Earth is made of several large subsystems, or spheres. These subsystems interact in a complex and always-changing whole that we can think of as the *Earth system*. Earth's subsystems include

- the geosphere, which is the mostly solid, rocky part of Earth
- the biosphere, which is living things and the areas of Earth where they are found
- the atmosphere, which is the layer of air surrounding Earth
- the hydrosphere, which is all of Earth's water

Oceans make up a large part of the hydrosphere because 97% of Earth's water is salt water.

Earth's subsystems can be seen from space.

19. Think about Earth's oceans as one subsystem within the larger Earth system. Describe at least two inputs and two outputs to the ocean subsystem. What are some interactions that the ocean has with other subsystems?

Convection Currents in the Ocean

The movement of matter due to differences in density is called **convection.** When denser material sinks, less dense material around it is pushed up. Convection also describes the transfer of energy due to the flow of matter. Convection can happen in gases, in liquids, and in solids that flow slowly. In the Earth system, convection happens in the atmosphere, in the ocean and other bodies of water, and in rock deep inside Earth. A convection current forms when convection happens repeatedly or in a cycle.

20. Add the following labels in the correct spaces below to complete
this general model of a convection current in the ocean:
- deep current moves toward equator
- surface current moves toward pole

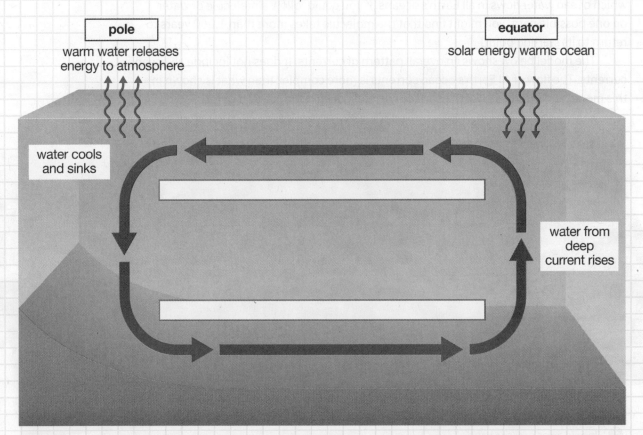

pole
warm water releases
energy to atmosphere

equator
solar energy warms ocean

water cools
and sinks

water from
deep
current rises

Convection currents involve the sinking of dense water and the rising of less dense
water in a circular path. This process takes place all over Earth's oceans to form global
circulation patterns. These patterns include surface currents that carry warm, less dense
water away from the equator toward the poles. Water from the deep ocean near the
equator rises to replace the water that is moving away on the surface. The patterns also
include deep ocean currents that carry cool, denser water away from the poles toward
the equator. These global circulation patterns affect the flow of energy and the cycling of
matter in the Earth system.

21. Language SmArts Using what you have read and observed in the diagram,
describe the path of a molecule of water in a convection current in the ocean.
Include a description of the transfers and transformations in energy that would
occur as the molecule travels in the convection current.

Global Ocean Circulation

When you put all the ocean currents together on a map or globe, you can see a pattern of water movement in the ocean. The model can be thought of as the main highway on which ocean water flows in all Earth's oceans. If you could follow a molecule of water on one possible path, you might find that the molecule takes more than 1,000 years to return to its starting point!

The model below shows an overall pattern of currents. It does not include all ocean currents. The flow of all Earth's ocean currents is more complex than what is shown in this model and includes all of the surface currents, deep currents, and gyres.

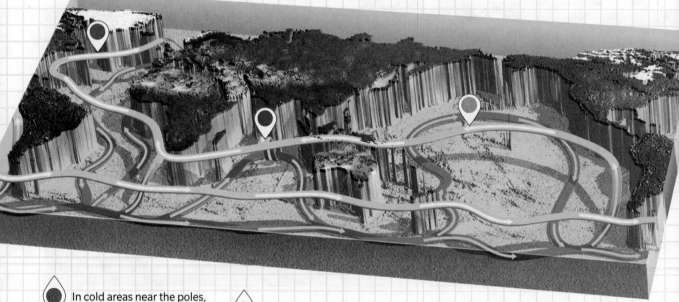

In cold areas near the poles, energy flows from the ocean into the atmosphere. The ocean water gets colder and more dense. This cooler, denser water sinks and then moves toward the equator along the ocean bottom.

In areas such as the Indian Ocean and the west coast of South America, deep water comes up to the surface. This upwelling of deep water brings cold, nutrient-rich water to the surface.

Near the equator, surface ocean water absorbs solar energy and gets warmer. This warm water tends to flow toward the poles and replace the cold water that is sinking there.

22. **Collaborate** In your school or community, there may be patterns of circulation that you can observe as groups of people move around during different times of the day. Work with a team to model these patterns with a map or drawing. Discuss with your team how the patterns you observe are like global ocean circulation and how they are different.

The Flow of Energy

Energy is transferred between the atmosphere and ocean water whenever the air and water are at different temperatures. When the air is warmer than the water, energy flows from the air to the water. When the water is warmer than the air, energy flows from the water to the air. These energy transfers happen all over the Earth system, and so the ocean has an important influence on weather and climate.

In addition to the transfer of energy back and forth between ocean water and the air, energy is transferred from the equator to polar areas by ocean currents. Near the equator, the ocean absorbs a huge amount of solar energy. It also absorbs energy from the air. Surface currents move this warm water toward the poles, where the energy is released into the colder air.

23. In which location would energy be transferred more quickly between the atmosphere and Earth's surface?

A. a lake where the air 5 °C

B. an ice sheet where the air 5 °C

24. Discuss Write an explanation for your answer choice. Discuss your explanation with a partner and cite evidence for your explanation.

The Cycling of Matter

Ocean currents transport not only energy but also matter in the Earth system. This matter includes the ocean water itself, dissolved solids such as salt, and gases such as oxygen and carbon dioxide. Matter transported by ocean currents also includes marine organisms such as plankton. Some substances transported by ocean currents are harmful to the environment. Human waste, garbage, and other pollutants can affect the environment in all the places to which ocean currents carry this pollution.

The cycling of matter in the Earth system also involves the chemical reactions and processes that take place in the ocean. For example, gases such as oxygen and carbon dioxide move back and forth between the ocean and the air depending on temperature, concentration of the gases, and other factors. Some marine organisms use carbon dioxide during the process of photosynthesis. During this process, organisms release oxygen into the water. The oxygen is then used by most living organisms during cellular respiration.

Diatoms are one type of plankton.

EVIDENCE NOTEBOOK

25. How might the cycling of matter in the ocean be related to the buildup of floating garbage in certain parts of the ocean? Why might some garbage float and not sink? Record your evidence.

The Carbon Cycle

This diagram shows the cycling of carbon through the Earth system, in living and nonliving subsystems. The ocean plays an important role in the carbon cycle.

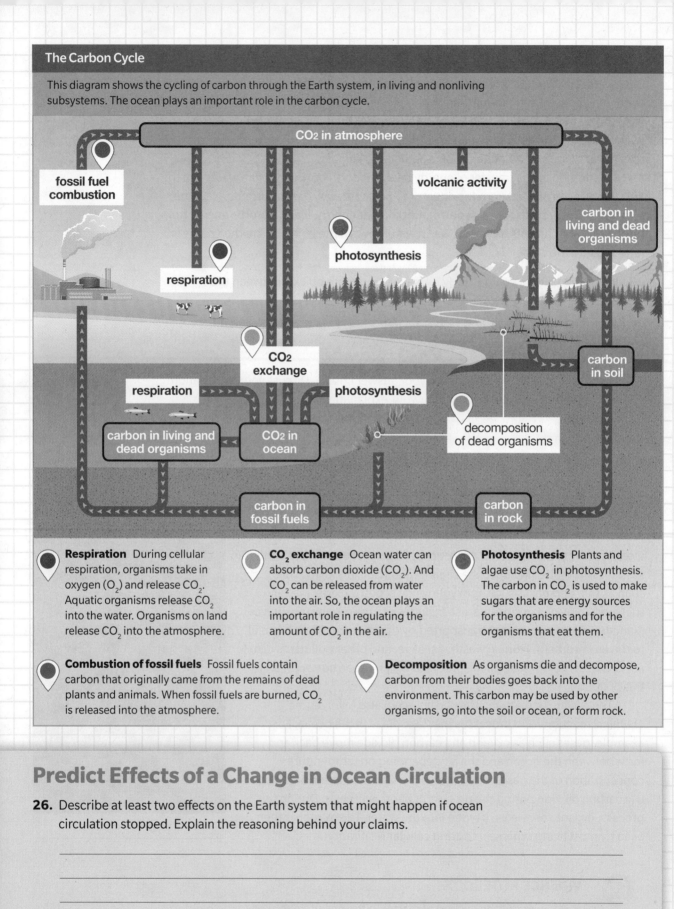

Respiration During cellular respiration, organisms take in oxygen (O_2) and release CO_2. Aquatic organisms release CO_2 into the water. Organisms on land release CO_2 into the atmosphere.

CO_2 exchange Ocean water can absorb carbon dioxide (CO_2). And CO_2 can be released from water into the air. So, the ocean plays an important role in regulating the amount of CO_2 in the air.

Photosynthesis Plants and algae use CO_2 in photosynthesis. The carbon in CO_2 is used to make sugars that are energy sources for the organisms and for the organisms that eat them.

Combustion of fossil fuels Fossil fuels contain carbon that originally came from the remains of dead plants and animals. When fossil fuels are burned, CO_2 is released into the atmosphere.

Decomposition As organisms die and decompose, carbon from their bodies goes back into the environment. This carbon may be used by other organisms, go into the soil or ocean, or form rock.

Predict Effects of a Change in Ocean Circulation

26. Describe at least two effects on the Earth system that might happen if ocean circulation stopped. Explain the reasoning behind your claims.

_____

_____

_____

_____

_____

Continue Your Exploration

Name: _____ **Date:** _____

Check out the path below or go online to choose one of the other paths shown.

Careers in Science

- **Hands-On Labs** ✋
- **Upwelling in Earth's Oceans**
- **Propose Your Own Path**

Go online to choose one of these other paths.

Physical Oceanographer

Oceanographers are scientists who study the ocean. There are many areas to study in oceanography. Some of these are marine ecosystems, ocean circulation, the geology of the sea floor, and the chemical and physical properties of ocean water. These topics are related. So it is important that oceanographers have an understanding of biology, chemistry, geology, and physics to unravel the mysteries of the ocean. All oceanographers must have a four-year college degree. Most go on to earn a master's degree and a doctorate before becoming ocean scientists.

One type of oceanographer, a physical oceanographer, studies the physical conditions and processes in the ocean. This involves studying phenomena such as waves, currents, and tides; the transport of sand on and off beaches; coastal erosion; and the interactions of the atmosphere and the ocean. Physical oceanographers also study the relationships that influence weather and climate, the behavior of light and sound in water, and the ocean's interactions with the sea floor.

1. Why is it important for physical oceanographers to have studied several different fields of science?

Oceanographers work outside *Alvin*, one of the world's first deep-sea submersibles. *Alvin* can take scientists as far as 4,500 meters below the ocean surface.

A physical oceanographer brings a CTD instrument onto a research ship. The CTD takes many measurements of conductivity, temperature, and depth.

Continue Your Exploration

2. Which descriptions identify areas of science that a physical oceanographer might need to use to answer questions about the topic listed? Choose all that apply.

   A. chemistry and physics to study how currents and salinity are related

   B. physics and geology to study the transport of sand on and off beaches

   C. biology, chemistry, geology, and physics to study the interactions of the atmosphere and the ocean

3. Write at least three questions that you could investigate if you were a physical oceanographer.

4. **Engineer It** Today physical oceanographers can measure the speed of ocean currents with up-to-date technology. For example, floating buoys that have Global Positioning System (GPS) devices can be used to collect data about where the buoy is traveling and how fast it is going. These data can be used to calculate the speed of a current and to map its direction. Before computers and GPS, scientists managed to map and measure currents with fair accuracy. Propose one way you could measure the speed of a surface ocean current if you had a boat you could anchor, pieces of wood, string or rope, and a stopwatch.

5. **Collaborate** With a partner, research and take notes about topics studied in a field of oceanography. Some fields to consider include marine biology, marine geology, and chemical oceanography. Compare your notes with a team that researched a different field. Predict how scientists from the different fields could collaborate in their research.

Can You Explain It?

Name: _____ Date: _____

Why does floating garbage tend to build up in certain places in the ocean?

Model shows predicted accumulation of floating garbage 10 years after release

EVIDENCE NOTEBOOK

Refer to the notes in your Evidence Notebook to help you construct an explanation for why floating garbage that comes mostly from the land tends to build up in certain places in the ocean.

1. State your claim. Make sure your claim fully explains how and why floating garbage builds up in certain areas.

2. Summarize the evidence you have gathered to support your claim and explain your reasoning.

Checkpoints

Answer the following questions to check your understanding of the lesson.

3. Which of the following would be the best choice to model what drives surface ocean currents?

   A. a tank of water with a block of ice attached to one end

   B. a tank of water with a fan blowing over the surface of the water

   C. a system of pipes with a heater at one end

   D. a tank of water with a heater under the tank

4. Fill in each blank with increases or decreases to show how the density of liquid ocean water can change.

   A. Rain falls into the ocean; the density of ocean water _____.

   B. Ocean water becomes colder; the density of ocean water _____.

   C. A river empties into the ocean; the density of ocean water _____.

Use the map to answer Question 5.

5. The map shows the surface temperature of the Gulf Stream and the ocean water farther north. Where are deep currents most likely to be forming as water from the surface sinks?

   A. south of 30° north latitude

   B. between 30° and 35° north latitude

   C. between 35° and 40° north latitude

   D. north of 40° north latitude

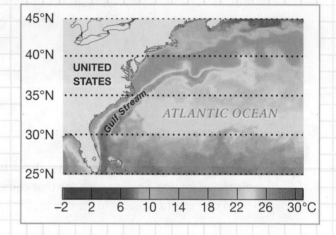

Use the map to answer Questions 6–7.

6. Which statement explains why the water in the South Pacific gyre begins to warm up as it moves away from the coast of South America?

   A. It receives more energy from the sun.

   B. It receives more rainfall from the atmosphere.

   C. It loses more heat energy to the atmosphere.

7. Ocean water in the cold / warm Peru current is deflected by the continent of South America / Australia and then joins the South Equatorial current.

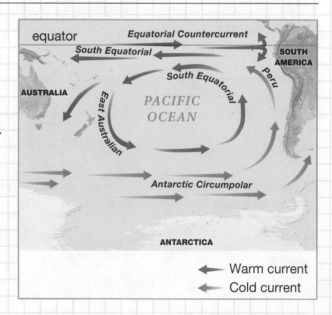

Interactive Review

Complete this section to review the main concepts of the lesson.

Surface currents are affected by wind, by the Coriolis effect, and by continental deflection.

A. Explain how energy that comes from outside the Earth system drives the flow of water in surface currents.

Deep ocean currents form when denser ocean water sinks. Deep currents are also affected by the Coriolis effect and by continental deflection.

B. Draw a diagram to show a model of one way a deep current could form.

Global ocean circulation moves water through Earth's ocean basins and plays an important role in the cycling of matter and the flow of energy in the Earth system.

C. Explain how the flow of matter and energy in global ocean circulation is related to interactions of the ocean with two other parts of the Earth system.

Scientific Visualization Studio (c) ©HMH/Steven Burr Williams; (b) ©Stocktrek Images, Inc./ Getty Images

The Water Cycle

A dark storm approaches a wooden structure built in the water in the Maldives.

By the end of this lesson . . .

you will learn how energy is involved in changing water's state and how water is constantly moving and cycling all over Earth.

CAN YOU EXPLAIN IT?

How could the water in a dinosaur's drink end up in a raindrop today?

Some of Earth's water makes up your body as well as the bodies of all living things. A tiny drop of water can contain more than a trillion water molecules. Every water molecule has its own story, and some water molecules at Earth's surface today may have been ingested by a dinosaur 200 million years ago.

1. Think about the last drink of water you took. How do you think that water may have moved or changed before you drank it?

2. How do you think the state of water affects its movement?

EVIDENCE NOTEBOOK As you explore the lesson, gather evidence to show how water in a dinosaur's drink could end up in a raindrop today.

Analyzing Water on Earth

Where Water Is Found on Earth

Water is found almost everywhere on Earth, and it exists in many forms. From space, it is easy to see Earth's oceans. They cover about 70% of Earth's surface. Salt water makes up about 97% of Earth's total volume of water. For humans and for many animals, the salt dissolved in seawater makes it too salty to drink. It is also too salty to use to water crops.

3. Together with a partner, look at the photo for evidence of water. Besides the oceans, where else is water present on Earth? Is it always in liquid form?

Earth is known as "the blue planet" because most of its surface is covered with water.

The Importance of Water on Earth

Water plays an important role in many processes in the Earth system. It shapes Earth's surface and influences weather. Water is also essential for life. You depend on clean, fresh drinking water to survive. Only a limited amount of Earth's water—about 2.5%—is fresh water. The remaining water on Earth is salt water. Almost 70% of Earth's fresh water is frozen in ice and not readily available for us to use. Therefore, it is important to protect our water resources.

Water's Role on Earth

Water shapes Earth's surface through weathering and erosion, and it also influences Earth's weather.

Water is vital for sustaining all organisms on Earth.

4. **Discuss** Together with a partner or with your class, discuss at least four things you did or used today that would not be possible or would not exist without water.

States of Water on Earth

Earth is the only planet in our solar system with abundant liquid water. The Earth system also contains water in two other states: gas and solid. Water (liquid), water vapor (an invisible gas), and ice (solid) all have the same chemical formula of H_2O.

The States of Water

Liquid Most of Earth's water is liquid. Gravity causes liquid water to flow downhill and rest in low-lying areas. As a result, Earth has rivers, lakes, and oceans.

Gas Most water vapor is in Earth's atmosphere. We cannot see water vapor, but our bodies take it in every time we inhale.

Solid Solid water forms ice crystals, snowflakes, and hail in Earth's atmosphere and ice and snow on Earth's surface.

5. Look at the scene in the photo. Describe two ways that the liquid water you see here could have come to this location on Earth.

Water's Changing State

When the temperature of the environment that water is in rises, water can absorb thermal energy. As water absorbs energy, it can change from solid to liquid, from liquid to gas, or from solid to gas. The same amount of water that existed before the change of state exists after the change of state.

On the other hand, if the surrounding environment cools, water can lose energy to its surroundings and can change state in the opposite direction. As energy is released from water, the water may change from gas to liquid, from liquid to solid, or from gas to solid.

 EVIDENCE NOTEBOOK

6. Think back to the dinosaur's drinking water. Was this water always in the liquid state? Did it remain in a liquid state after the dinosaur drank it? Record your evidence.

7. In each image, fill in the blank to indicate whether water _gains_ or _loses_ energy.

Water ___gains___ energy.

As air temperatures increase, the water molecules in this ice begin to vibrate just enough to break free and start to flow past one another to form a liquid.

Water _____ energy.

As air temperatures decrease, the molecules in liquid water begin to move more slowly until they only vibrate in place. The molecules form the rigid structure of solid water, or ice.

Water _____ energy.

As air temperatures increase, liquid water molecules begin to vibrate enough that some will escape the liquid's surface into the air above as water vapor.

Water _____ energy.

As water vapor molecules rise, they eventually enter colder air. This causes the molecules to vibrate at a slower rate and change to liquid water droplets.

Do the Math
Analyze Temperatures

The freezing point and the melting point of water are both 0 °C. If water cools to 0 °C or below, it is likely to freeze. If ice warms to 0 °C or above, it is likely to melt. And the boiling point of water is 100 °C.

8. In the United States and some other countries, temperature is generally measured in degrees Fahrenheit (°F). Scientists generally measure temperature in degrees Celsius (°C), so it is helpful to be familiar with both temperature scales. Use the equation to calculate the temperature in °F for each item shown in the photos. The first one has been done for you.

$$F = \frac{9}{5}C + 32$$

a running stream

25 °C = ___77 °F___

snow

0 °C = _____

boiling water

100 °C = _____

Describing the Movement of Water in Earth's Atmosphere

Earth's Atmosphere

A mixture of gases surrounds Earth and makes up its atmosphere. Earth's atmosphere contains nitrogen, carbon dioxide, oxygen, and water. At any given time there is about 12,900 km^3 of water in the atmosphere. That's enough to water to completely fill Lake Superior, the largest lake by volume in North America!

The atmosphere contains a lot of water vapor, which you cannot see.

9. What evidence of water in the atmosphere can you see in the photo?

How Water Reaches the Atmosphere

Water can exist in the atmosphere as a solid, a liquid, and a gas. In addition to evaporation, two other processes can move water into the atmosphere from Earth's surface. These processes are transpiration and sublimation.

10. Where can water in the atmosphere come from? Circle all possible answers.

    A. oceans

    B. plants

    C. ice

    D. puddles

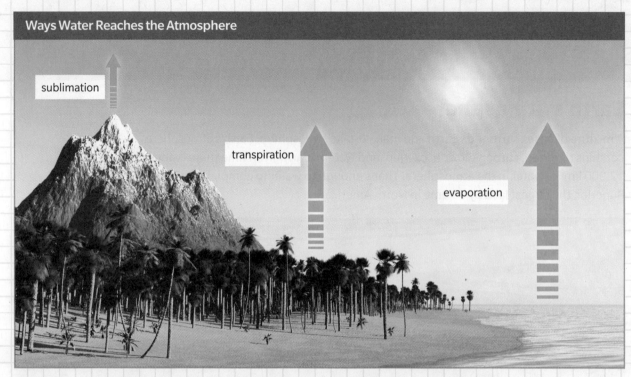

Ways Water Reaches the Atmosphere

sublimation

transpiration

evaporation

When solid water changes directly to water vapor without first becoming a liquid, the process is called **sublimation**. Energy is required for this process to occur because the molecules of the solid water must gain energy to break free from the solid.

Liquid water is found in organisms' bodies. Water is ingested as an animal eats and drinks. Some water is stored in the animal's body and some is returned back into the environment by excretion or respiration. When an animal dies, its body decomposes and any water in the body is returned to the environment. Like many organisms, plants release water vapor into the environment. As water flows throughout a plant, some water changes to water vapor as it leaves the plant through small openings called stomata. This release of water vapor into the air by plants is called **transpiration**. This process requires the addition of energy to the water molecules, so they can break away from the liquid state.

When liquid water gains enough energy to escape the liquid's surface and form water vapor, the process is called **evaporation**. Some water evaporates from the water on land. However, most water evaporates from the surface of Earth's oceans.

How important are the contributions from each source of atmospheric water? About 90% of the water in the atmosphere comes from evaporation of Earth's liquid water, especially oceans. About 10% of the water in the atmosphere comes from transpiration. Less than 1% of the water in the atmosphere comes from sublimation.

Water in the Atmosphere

Water molecules in the atmosphere are in constant motion, bouncing against each other and against other gas molecules in the air. During these collisions, the water molecules can gain or lose energy. If a water molecule collides with a molecule that is warmer than it is, the water molecule will gain energy. If a water molecule collides with a molecule that is cooler, the water molecule will lose energy.

 EVIDENCE NOTEBOOK

11. Through what processes might the water have changed and moved before and after the dinosaur drank it? Record your evidence.

Hands-On Lab
Model the Formation of Clouds and Rain

You will model Earth's atmosphere inside a jar.

Procedure and Analysis

STEP 1 Carefully fill a jar about half full by pouring 250 mL of hot water into it.

STEP 2 Place a dented lid on top of the jar so that it covers the entire opening and the raised bumps are facing down into the jar.

STEP 3 Place ice cubes, a little cold water, and a teaspoon of salt into the can and stir. Put the cold can on top of the lid of the jar.

STEP 4 Shine a flashlight through the jar. Record your observations. Repeat this step every few minutes for 10 minutes.

MATERIALS
- can, empty
- flashlight
- ice cubes
- glass jar, medium size with a dented lid
- salt (1 tsp)
- water, very hot (250 mL)
- water, cold

STEP 5 Use what you observed in this activity to explain some of the things that can happen to water in Earth's atmosphere. What might cause these changes?

Condensation and Clouds

As air cools, water vapor in the air may change to liquid water. The process of a gas becoming a liquid is called **condensation**. As water molecules bump into each other, they can stick together and form small water droplets or ice crystals, depending on the air temperature. At first, these droplets form around tiny particles in the air, such as sea salt, dust, and pollen. As more and more water molecules collect in the water droplets, the droplets become larger. Eventually, there may be enough water droplets to form visible clouds, fog, or mist.

High clouds that form at temperatures colder than those close to Earth's surface are made up of solid ice crystals and liquid droplets. At the ground level, water vapor may condense as dew or frost on cool surfaces, such as blades of grass and windows.

12. Microscopic droplets of water in the air grow larger as water vapor continues to condense. What might happen next?

Precipitation

As the water droplets in clouds become larger and larger, gravity continually pulls the water droplets toward Earth's surface. **Precipitation** is any form of water that falls to Earth from clouds. Three common kinds of precipitation are rain, snow, and hail. Snow and hail form if the water in clouds freezes.

Hail stones are frozen balls of precipitation that form in some thunderstorms.

You can see the beautiful six-part crystals of snowflakes when they are viewed under magnification.

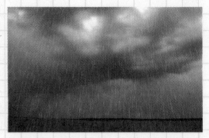

Rain falls when water droplets that form in clouds are pulled to Earth's surface by gravity.

Deposition

Deposition occurs when water vapor changes state directly from a gas to a solid. Deposition is the reverse of sublimation. One example of deposition occurs high in the atmosphere or on the top of high mountains where the temperature is very low. In these conditions, water vapor forms snow without becoming a liquid first.

13. Circle the best answer to complete each statement.

    A. When water vapor in the atmosphere condenses and forms water droplets, the water molecules *absorb / release* energy.

    B. When water droplets in the atmosphere form ice crystals, the water molecules *absorb / release* energy.

Describe the Formation of Hail

Sometimes, when ice crystals form in clouds and begin to fall, strong winds carry the ice crystals high into the clouds. When the crystals begin falling again, they grow larger as more water droplets freeze onto them. Clumps of ice, called hailstones, start to form. Eventually, the hailstones grow too heavy for the wind to carry and they fall to Earth.

14. Describe a time during the formation of hailstones when water releases energy.

_____

_____

_____

_____

Describing the Movement of Water on Earth's Surface

Much of Earth's surface is covered with water. Most of this water is salt water, which makes up Earth's oceans, salt marshes, and salty lakes. Only a small amount of Earth's water is fresh water, and most of that is frozen as sea ice at the poles or as ice and snow on land.

15. Can you see all the locations of fresh water on Earth in photos of Earth's surface? Explain.

The Dungeness River in Washington State forks before entering the bay and the Strait of Juan de Fuca.

Ocean Circulation

While it is easy to observe water flowing on land after a rainstorm, remember that most of Earth's precipitation falls into the ocean. Just as water moves through Earth's rivers, water in the ocean also moves in patterns. The movement of ocean water in a particular direction and pattern is called a *current*. This diagram shows the main pattern of ocean circulation, but does not show all ocean currents. The light green paths show currents on the ocean surface. The dark green paths show currents below the surface.

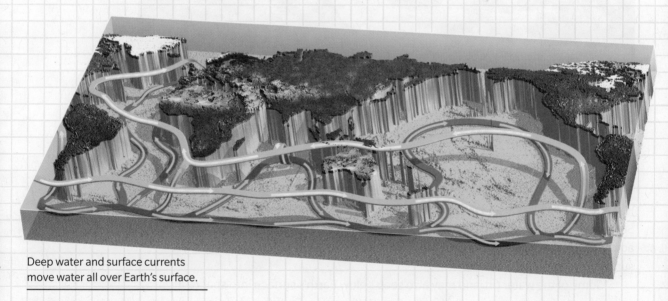

Deep water and surface currents move water all over Earth's surface.

16. In which ways might ocean currents be like streams and rivers on land?

Surface Currents and Deep Ocean Currents

Currents at or near the ocean surface are called *surface currents*. Surface currents are powered by wind. The Gulf Stream that moves warm ocean water from the Gulf of Mexico northeast toward Europe is one example of a surface current.

Currents that flow below the ocean surface are called *deep currents*. These currents are driven by differences in water densities that cause water to sink below surrounding water in some parts of the ocean.

Deep currents flow at all levels of the ocean below the surface. Ocean currents transport large amounts of water as well as dissolved solids, dissolved gases, organisms, and energy around the Earth system.

Water Movement on Land

Water from the atmosphere falls to Earth's surface in the form of precipitation. Some precipitation forms coverings of snow and ice on mountains and other cold places. When this ice and snow melt, and when rain falls, the liquid water flows downhill. Some of the water may seep into the ground.

In the Highlands of Scotland, mountain streams flow down to lower elevations.

17. What might happen to water after it seeps into the ground?

Runoff and Infiltration

Just as gravity pulls you and all other objects toward Earth's center, it also pulls on water. So, when precipitation lands on Earth's surface, some of the water will flow downhill across Earth's surface into wetlands, rivers, or lakes. Water that flows across Earth's surface this way is called **runoff**.

Some of the water on land may also seep below Earth's surface into spaces in soil and rock. This process is called *infiltration*. Water under Earth's surface is called *groundwater*. Groundwater can flow downhill through soil and some types of rock. Some drinking water in the United States comes from groundwater supplies. To use these supplies, people drill down into the ground to reach the groundwater. More than half of Earth's fresh water exists as ice and about a third exists as groundwater.

Water Movement on and below Earth's Surface

Water flows over Earth's surface as runoff from precipitation and melting snow and ice. Some of this water flows through streams and rivers. Some of this water seeps downward to form groundwater.

Explore ONLINE!

18. Which statement correctly describes the movement of water represented by arrows in the picture? Choose all that apply.

   A. Water from melting snow runs down the mountainside.

   B. Rainwater seeps into the ground.

   C. Streams carry water to the mountain peaks.

   D. Gravity prevents groundwater from reaching Earth's surface.

19. Engineer It In some rivers and lakes, dams are constructed to harvest energy by converting the kinetic energy of moving water into electrical energy. Water from behind the dam flows through a turbine that transforms kinetic energy into mechanical energy. The turbine turns a generator that converts mechanical energy into electrical energy.

   The water from behind the dam could flow to the turbine either through an opening near the middle or top of the dam or by flowing over the top of the dam. Which type of water flow would be the best design for sending a consistent flow of water past the turbines? Explain your reasoning.

Dams, such as the Glen Canyon Dam, can help control water movement on Earth's surface.

Ice on Earth's Surface

Most of Earth's solid fresh water is locked up in large ice caps in Antarctica and Greenland or in ice floating in polar ocean water. Some ice is also found in glaciers. Glaciers are sometimes called "rivers of ice" because gravity causes them to move slowly downhill. Many glaciers never leave land. However, some glaciers reach the ocean, where pieces may break off and form icebergs.

20. How might an iceberg move once it breaks off from a glacier?

Glacier Bay National Park, Alaska, is home to large glaciers that have piled up ice on land for thousands of years. This glacier flows to the ocean.

Analyze Processes

21. Which of the following processes could have caused this cave to fill with water?

   A. evaporation

   B. sublimation

   C. infiltration

   D. transpiration

22. Together with a partner, think of a way water might exit this cave. Explain your reasoning.

A limestone cave beneath Earth's surface can fill with water over time.

_____

_____

_____

_____

_____

_____

_____

Modeling the Water Cycle

You can use everyday experiences to observe and model the movement of water in Earth's systems. You can observe some changes in water after any hot shower you take. While much of the shower water goes down the drain, some evaporates into the bathroom air. You know this because the mirror fogs up as that water vapor condenses back into liquid. When returning to the bathroom after a day at school, you notice that the mirror and your wet towel are now dry. Think about what may have happened to the water.

Time

23. **Discuss** Together with a partner, examine the photos. The material inside the glass changes over time. What do you think happened? Did the ice and water just disappear?

The Water Cycle

On a global scale, water constantly moves through the Earth system. The movement of water between the atmosphere, land, oceans, and living things is called the **water cycle**. This cycling of water involves changes of state, the movement of water in different forms, and the transfer of matter and energy in the Earth system.

A Water Cycle Model

24. Complete the water cycle model by writing the correct process in the spaces provided. Write *condensation*, *runoff*, *infiltration*, or *evaporation*.

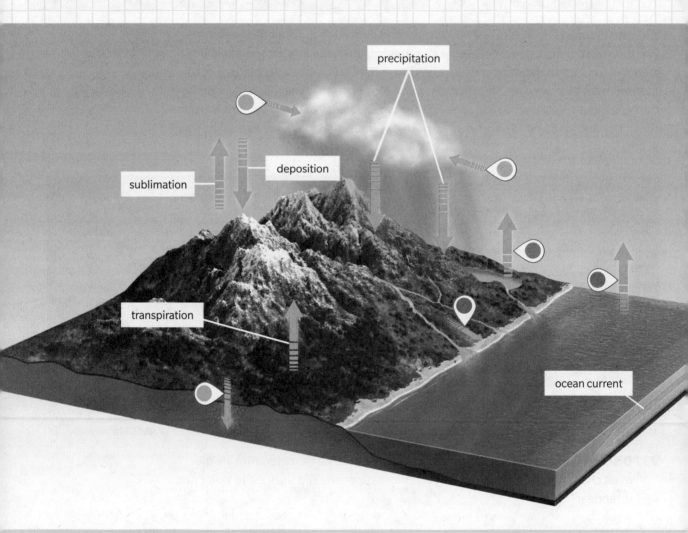

○ <u>condensation</u>   ◉ <u>Run-off</u>
● <u>evaporation</u>   ◉ <u>infiltration</u>

25. What other processes that involve water in the Earth system are not shown in this model of the water cycle?

Sunlight and Gravity Drive the Water Cycle

Surface water, groundwater, and ice flow downhill because of gravity. And precipitation falls to Earth's surface because of gravity. Energy from the sun is the source of energy for changes of state in which water absorbs energy, such as melting and evaporation. Solar energy also powers Earth's winds, which move air and water in the atmosphere.

26. Describe what might happen in the water cycle if the amount of solar energy entering the Earth system decreased.

The Flow of Energy in the Water Cycle

Energy flows through the Earth system in the water cycle in two ways—when water changes state and when water moves from place to place. When water changes state, water molecules absorb energy from or release energy to their surroundings. For example, evaporating water absorbs energy from sunlight or from surrounding air, water, or land. When water condenses to form clouds, the water molecules release energy to the surrounding atmosphere.

As water moves, it transfers energy from one location to another. For example, as a warm surface current in the ocean flows to a colder polar region, thermal energy from the equator is transported toward Earth's poles. The cooling water releases thermal energy into the atmosphere. These energy transfers between the ocean and atmosphere greatly influence Earth's weather and climate.

27. Imagine snow on top of a mountain. Describe at least two ways energy could be transferred as the seasons change.

The Cycling of Matter in the Water Cycle

As water moves above, on top of, and below Earth's surface, it carries other matter with it. For example, streams and rivers carry sand, mud, and living things, which are deposited in a new place. As water moves over land, some substances will dissolve in the water and be carried along with it. When the water evaporates, the dissolved substances will be deposited. Precipitation can carry substances from the air to the ground, including gases, dust, ash, pollen, and pollutants.

28. What are some examples of the cycling of matter that happen as a result of the water cycle? Choose all answers that apply.

    A. Raindrops carry dissolved gases from the air to Earth's surface.

    B. Rivers carve valleys and canyons.

    C. Rivers move water to the ocean.

    D. Runoff moves pollutants from one place to another on Earth's surface.

29. How could a water molecule be transferred and transformed through the water cycle over millions of years? Record your evidence.

Model the Water Cycle

The movement of water throughout Earth's systems is called the water cycle. However, this cycle is not a "circle" of events. A water molecule can take different paths as it moves through the cycle. The term *cycle* refers to the fact that water continuously moves from Earth's surface to the atmosphere and back.

30. Language SmArts Remember the water on the bathroom mirror that appears after you take a shower? Tell a story about how those droplets appear on the mirror and what could happen to a water molecule from one of the droplets as it moves through the water cycle. Describe at least four changes in the state of water, the processes that move the water, and how energy flows to and from the water. Be sure to include at least one living organism in the water cycle.

_____

_____

_____

_____

_____

_____

_____

31. Draw In the space below, draw a model to go with your story. Use arrows and labels to show processes in the water cycle. Present your story and model to the class.

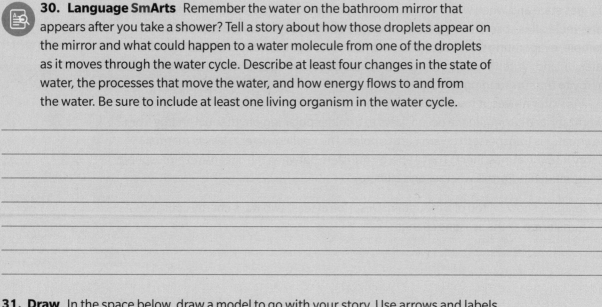

Continue Your Exploration

Name: _____   Date: _____

Check out the path below or go online to choose one of the other paths shown.

| Careers in Science | • **Hands-On Labs** 🖐
 • **Investigating Water Sources**
 • **Propose Your Own Path** | Go online to choose one of these other paths. |

Hydrologist

Hydrologists are scientists who study water. They study a wide variety of topics, including water quality and availability. Some hydrologists also study water's movement at different scales, from global ocean currents to local replenishment of reservoirs by spring snowmelt. Hydrologists use many instruments in their work, including depth gauges and flow meters.

Hydrologists take water samples along irrigation channels near the Rio Grande. They are looking for pharmaceuticals, nutrients, metals, and other characteristics to determine water quality.

Continue Your Exploration

The Rio Grande runs along the border between Texas, in the United States, and Mexico. The river is an important resource. It is a vital stop along birds' migration routes, is central to many important desert ecosystems, and houses several dams used for purposes such as generating electrical energy and diverting water to irrigate cropland. However, the Rio Grande is polluted from human activities. Its water levels have significantly declined over the past century from human activities and changes in climate. Hydrologists play an important role in collecting data that show how much water runs through the river, how much water is used for different human activities, and what pollutants are in the water.

1. A hydrologist needs to know how much water will run off into a river in the spring after an exceptionally snowy winter. What data will the hydrologist need to consider? Choose all that apply.

    A. air temperature

    B. amount of precipitation in the winter

    C. depth of snowpack on surrounding mountain peaks

    D. stream flow rates

    E. reservoir water depth

2. Why is the work of hydrologists important?

3. What type of information about water and the water cycle would be important for a hydrologist to focus on in your community?

4. **Collaborate** Work with a small group to list the sources of drinking water in your community, such as lakes, rivers, and reservoirs. Think about why that source was chosen for use. Then consider a scenario that could reduce the amount of clean, fresh water available to the residents of the community. Together, "think like a hydrologist" to describe the scenario and to make predictions about the outcome. Create a brochure to provide to the community explaining the situation.

Can You Explain It?

Name: _____   Date: _____

How could the water in a dinosaur's drink end up in a raindrop today?

EVIDENCE NOTEBOOK

Refer to the notes in your Evidence Notebook to help you construct an explanation for how some of the water molecules in a dinosaur's drink could be the very same ones in a raindrop today.

1. State your claim. Make sure your claim fully explains how the water molecules in a raindrop falling today also could have been ingested by a dinosaur millions of years ago.

2. Summarize the evidence you have gathered to support your claim and explain your reasoning.

Checkpoints

Answer the following questions to check your understanding of the lesson.
Use the photo to answer Questions 3–5.

3. What state(s) of water do you directly observe in this photo? Choose all that apply.

   A. liquid

   B. solid

   C. gas

4. As the snow forms in the atmosphere, the water molecules *gain / lose / neither gain nor lose* energy.

5. How will the environment shown in the photo change when summer arrives? Select all that apply.

   A. The snow will melt.

   B. The water will evaporate from the stream.

   C. Transpiration could occur.

   D. Snow will continue to fall and form large piles.

Use the photo to answer Questions 6–8.

6. Which of the following steps of the water cycle can you infer are taking place in this scene at the moment the photo was taken? Choose all that apply.

   A. evaporation

   B. sublimation

   C. condensation

   D. transpiration

7. Using numbers 1-4, order the following events in a sequence that most logically describes the movement of water from the ocean to the bottom of a well in a village on the island.

   _____ condensation

   _____ infiltration

   _____ evaporation

   _____ precipitation

8. Water in the clouds in this scene eventually moves from the atmosphere to the land by *infiltration / precipitation / evaporation*.

   Next, *transpiration / melting / runoff* carries that water to the sea.

   Wind / Gravity drives both examples of water movement.

Interactive Review

Complete this section to review the main concepts of the lesson.

The water on Earth can be found in three states: as a solid, a liquid, and a gas.

A. What causes water to change state? Explain by using an example.

Water in the atmosphere affects cloud formation and precipitation.

B. Use a sequence of at least four events to describe some of the ways that water moves into, through, and then out of the atmosphere.

Water moves on Earth's surface, below Earth's surface, and in Earth's oceans.

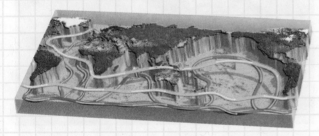

C. Make a table to describe at least one way that water moves in each of these parts of the Earth system: in the oceans, above ground, and below ground.

Water molecules can follow many different paths through the water cycle.

D. Explain the roles of sunlight and gravity in the water cycle.

Choose one of the activities to explore how this unit connects to other topics.

☐ Environmental Science Connection

Crocodile Surfers! The estuarine crocodile is the world's largest living reptile. It occupies many South Pacific islands. However, these crocodiles are poor swimmers. So how were they able to colonize islands that are so far apart? A group of Australian ecologists have a theory that the crocodiles ride ocean currents, like a surfer catching a wave!

Research and answer the questions: *How can crocodiles use ocean currents to travel long distances? What role do ocean currents play in their migration? How did scientists figure this out?* Then make a multimedia presentation to share what you learned with your class.

☐ Life Science Connection

Sleep Flying? During migration, frigatebirds follow expected flight patterns, circling on thermal air columns to fly high into the sky, and then gliding back down in straight lines. Air movement makes this possible. Amazingly, researchers have realized that these birds can sleep while flying!

Research and answer the questions: *How can frigatebirds sleep while flying? How did scientists figure this out? What role do air currents play in their migration?* Then make a multimedia presentation to share what you learned with your class.

☐ Art Connection

Water as Art Water has inspired art for hundreds of years. The French impressionist painter Claude Monet is known for his paintings of water lilies. Katsushika Hokusai's famous image *The Great Wave* shows a much different form of liquid water.

Select an art piece that has water. For this piece of art, identify the visible and invisible states of matter. Use visuals to explain how gravity and energy from the sun would cycle the water in these art pieces.

The Japanese Footbridge, by Claude Monet, 1899

Name: _____   Date: _____

Complete this review to check your understanding of the unit.

Use the diagram to answer Questions 1–3.

1. What process does this image show?

   A. condensation

   B. carbon cycling

   C. convection

   D. Coriolis Effect

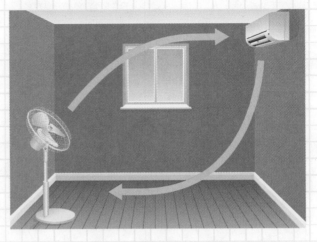

2. Which of the following is a strength of this model?

   A. Arrows are used to show movement of air.

   B. Explanations of the unseen mechanisms are included.

   C. The relationships between energy, gravity, and cycling are labeled.

   D. The model can be used to predict more processes related to air movement.

3. How could you plan an investigation that would let you better understand the model? Select all that apply.

   A. Develop a procedure to measure the speed of air movement and temperature at multiple spots in the room.

   B. Take photographs throughout the day and compare the images.

   C. Add streamers to the fan and air conditioner to show where the air is moving.

   D. Cover the window with a dark cloth and measure the solar energy with a ruler.

Use the diagram to answer Questions 4–5.

4. Which processes are missing from this model of the water cycle? Select all that apply.

   A. sublimation

   B. transpiration

   C. evaporation

   D. precipitation

5. What labels would you add to this model to show how gravity drives water cycling between the Earth's surface and the atmosphere?

   A. evaporation on the surface of the water

   B. precipitation falling from the clouds to the water

   C. air current circulation

   D. ocean current circulation

6. Complete the table by describing how each factor involved in the circulation of Earth's air and water relates to each big concept.

Factor	Energy and Matter	System Models	Patterns
Earth's Atmosphere	Moving air transfers energy and matter. As air is heated near the surface, it forms a low pressure area. The warmer air moves up as colder, denser air pushes it up and away.		
Earth's Oceans			
Force of Gravity			
Energy from the Sun			

Name: _____   Date: _____

Use the photo of dry ice to answer Questions 7–10.

7. Identify the change of state that is occurring.

8. Describe the transfers of energy required to cause this change of state.

9. Where in nature might you expect to observe this process?

10. Describe how this process would fit into a model or diagram of the water cycle.

Use the map to answer Questions 11–14.

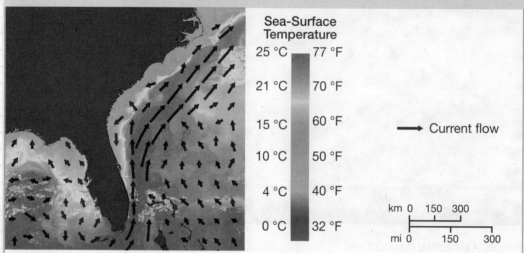

Florida Ocean Currents

This map shows the direction of the current flow and the temperature of the surface water around the coast of Florida.

Sea-Surface Temperature

25 °C	77 °F
21 °C	70 °F
15 °C	60 °F
10 °C	50 °F
4 °C	40 °F
0 °C	32 °F

→ Current flow

km 0   150   300
mi 0   150   300

Credit: Adapted from "The Florida Current" from Ocean Surface Currents. Reprinted by permission of Professor Arthur J. Mariano.
Source: NOAA Ocean Explorer, Islands in the Stream, 2001; University of Miami, Surface Currents in the Atlantic Ocean, 2001–2013

11. What can you tell about the currents around Florida from looking at this map?

12. What patterns and relationships do you observe in water temperature, latitude, current direction, and the shape of the continent?

13. The strong current shown on the map is called the Gulf Stream. What effect do you think the Gulf Stream has on the climate of the eastern United States and Western Europe?

14. Your friend who lives in Tennessee does not think he needs to know about ocean currents because they do not affect his community. Do you agree? Explain.

Name: _____   Date: _____

Should we build a dam?

A community has proposed building a dam on a major river. The dam could supply farmers with enough irrigation water for farming. Electrical energy could also be generated by this dam. Consider the possible consequences and benefits of this dam, and make a recommendation about whether or not the dam should be built.

Proposed Dam Site on the Savannah River

This map shows all the dams that have been built on the Savannah River and the proposed location of the new dam.

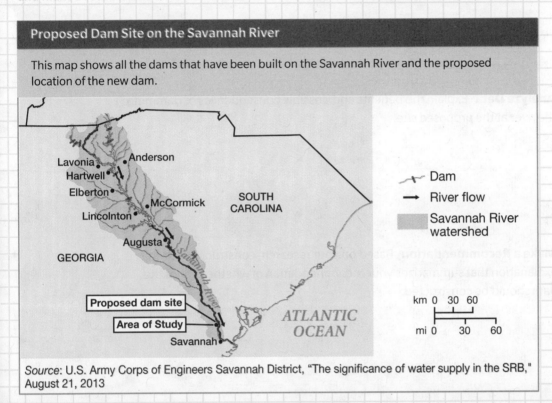

Source: U.S. Army Corps of Engineers Savannah District, "The significance of water supply in the SRB," August 21, 2013

The steps below will help guide your research and develop your recommendation.

Engineer It

1. **Ask a Question** Develop questions you will need to answer to determine how the dam will affect the community and environment. Research how other dams have impacted the communities around them.

Engineer It

2. **Conduct Research** Conduct research to answer the questions you identified in Step 1. Explain how each of the potential consequences you identified would affect people, the nonliving environment, and living things other than humans.

3. **Analyze Data** Explain the benefits and possible consequences of damming the river at the proposed site.

4. **Make a Recommendation** Based on your research, construct a written explanation that summarizes your recommendation of whether or not the dam should be constructed.

5. **Communicate** Present your recommendation to your class. Your presentation should include a model and other evidence that support your claims.

Self-Check

		I defined the problems that damming the river could cause and solve.
		I researched and learned the possible consequences of damming a river.
		My recommendation was based on evidence gathered from research and on the analysis of data.
		My recommendation was clearly communicated to others.

Weather and Climate

Hurricanes may start small with light winds, but they can quickly grow to include powerful winds and heavy rain that can cause serious damage to structures on land.

Weather has a large impact on our lives. It influences which activities we do during our day, what we wear, and how well food and crops that we eat will grow. Sometimes, weather conditions can become extreme. Luckily, there are ways to predict patterns of weather. In this unit, you will investigate the processes of weather and how weather can be predicted, as well as how it relates to climate.

Why It Matters

Here are some questions to consider as you work through the unit. Can you answer any of the questions now? Revisit these questions at the end of the unit to apply what you discover.

Questions	Notes
How does weather affect your daily life?	
How can weather predictions help you prepare for emergencies and keep you safe?	
Why would you look at a weather forecast for an upcoming week?	
How would you describe the climate where you live?	
What things would you consider if you moved somewhere that has a different climate?	
Do you eat different foods at different times of the year? What factors determine what you eat and when you eat it?	

Unit Starter: Identifying Locations and Latitude

Latitude is a measure of relative position north or south of the equator on the surface of the Earth. It is measured in degrees from the equator, which has a latitude of 0°. Both poles have a latitude of 90°, but the North Pole is at 90° north and the South Pole is at 90° south.

1. What is the latitude of each city? Fill in the correct latitude in the box next to each city.

0.2° S
12.5° S
33.9° S
4.7° N
28.6° N
~~59.3° N~~

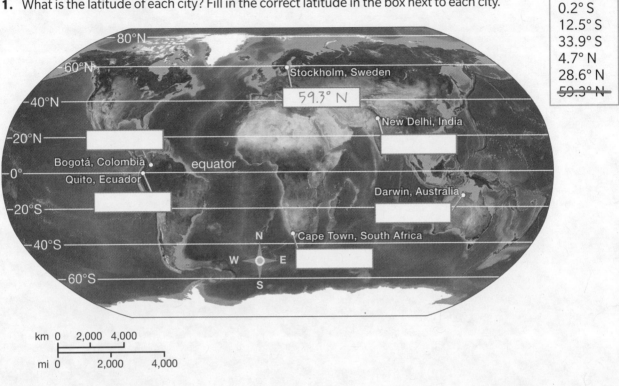

Stockholm, Sweden: 59.3° N

2. Which city is closest to the equator?

A. Stockholm, Sweden

B. New Delhi, India

C. Bogotá, Colombia

D. Darwin, Australia

E. Cape Town, South Africa

F. Quito, Ecuador

Go online to download the Unit Project Worksheet to help you plan your project.

Unit Project

Investigating Severe Weather

What factors cause severe weather? Choose a region of the world and a type of severe weather that affects that region. Develop and use a climate model to explain the factors in the atmosphere and ocean that cause the severe weather. Include in your model any characteristics of the region that affect the severe weather patterns.

Influences on Weather

Heavy rain is pouring down from this storm cloud. Where do you think the clouds and rain came from?

By the end of this lesson . . .

you will be able to explain how air masses interact and cause changes in weather.

Go online to view the digital version of the Hands-On Lab for this lesson and to download additional lab resources.

CAN YOU EXPLAIN IT?

What could cause a storm like this to happen suddenly?

It was a calm and cloudy spring day in this Utah town. Suddenly the clouds grew dark and heavy, and a storm covered the town in a blanket of snow.

Explore ONLINE!

1. What could cause the weather to change suddenly like this?

2. **Draw** Include a drawing to illustrate your explanation.

EVIDENCE NOTEBOOK As you explore this lesson, gather evidence to help explain what causes sudden changes in weather like this storm.

Describing Weather

Elements of Weather

Has weather ever caused your plans to change? **Weather** is a description of the short-term conditions of the atmosphere at a particular time and place. Reports of weather might include information about temperature, humidity, precipitation, air pressure, wind speed, and cloud cover.

3. What is the weather like right now? What is your favorite kind of weather? What is your least favorite kind of weather?

Temperature

Temperature is a measure of how hot or cold something is, which has to do with the motion of the particles that make up matter. So, air temperature is related to how fast air particles are moving. Look at the diagrams. When air particles have more energy, they move faster and the temperature is greater.

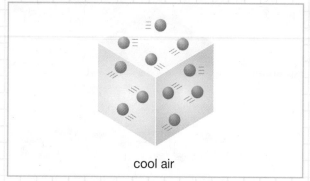

cool air

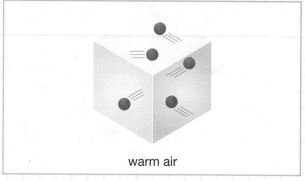

warm air

This is a model of cool air particles in a cube. The cool air particles move slowly.

In the same volume of warm air, the particles move faster and are more spread out. Warm air is less dense than cool air.

Humidity

Humidity is a measure of the amount of water vapor in the air. Much of the water vapor in air comes from the evaporation of liquid water on Earth's surface. The more water vapor there is in the air, the higher the humidity of the air is. Humidity affects how warm or cool you feel. You might feel comfortable at 25 °C, but if the humidity rises, you may feel too warm, even though the temperature is the same.

Weather reports often refer to relative humidity. *Relative humidity* is the percentage of water vapor in air relative to the amount needed to saturate the air at the same temperature. For example, at 10 °C, air becomes saturated when there are 8 grams of water vapor per kilogram of air (g/kg). At this point, the relative humidity is 100%. If there were only 4 g/kg of water vapor in the air at 10 °C, then the relative humidity would be 50%. The warmer the air is, the more water vapor it can contain without reaching saturation.

Clouds and Precipitation

What happens when relative humidity exceeds 100%? At this point, more water vapor condenses than evaporates. The water vapor condenses onto particles in the air, such as dust and pollen, to form liquid water droplets or ice crystals. These droplets and crystals form clouds. The droplets and ice crystals in clouds fall back to Earth as precipitation, such as rain, snow, hail, or sleet. The type of precipitation that forms and falls depends on the air temperature where the cloud formed and the changing air temperature as the precipitation falls to the ground.

Clouds themselves affect the air temperature. During the day, clouds can keep an area cool by reflecting more sunlight back into space. Clouds also affect temperatures overnight. Earth's surface radiates heat. If no clouds are present, much of the heat escapes into space. If clouds are present, they radiate heat back down to Earth's surface. This is why a cloudy night is often warmer than a clear night.

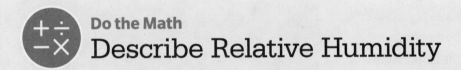

Do the Math
Describe Relative Humidity

The line on this graph shows how much water vapor is in the air at 100% relative humidity at different temperatures. For example, at 30 °C, relative humidity reaches 100% when there are 29 g of water in each kilogram of air.

4. Use the graph to circle the word that correctly completes each sentence.

   A. As temperature increases, it takes more / less water vapor to reach 100% relative humidity.

   B. At 25 °C with 10 g/kg of water vapor in the air, precipitation is likely / not likely.

   C. If 10 g/kg of water vapor remained in the air and the temperature dropped to 10 °C, precipitation would be likely / not likely.

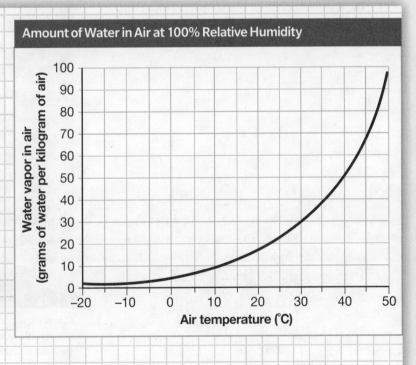

Amount of Water in Air at 100% Relative Humidity

Graph: Water vapor in air (grams of water per kilogram of air) vs. Air temperature (°C)

5. Think about the storm that swept over the town in Utah. How did the clouds and snow form? Record your evidence.

Air Pressure

Particles of air are invisible, but they do have mass. Gravity pulls the particles toward Earth's surface. Air particles press on objects from all sides. *Air pressure* is the force of air pushing on an object. The air pressure on any one object on Earth depends on how much air exists above that object. The more air above an object, the greater the air pressure will be. Air pressure is measured in millibars (mb). At sea level, the air pressure is about 1,013 mb. Higher above sea level, less air is above you, so the air pressure will be less. For example, the air pressure on the top of Mount Everest is only 300 mb.

6. A student drank a bottle of water during a car ride up a mountain. At the top of the mountain, the student capped the plastic bottle. During the drive back down the mountain, what might happen to the bottle?

   A. It will expand because the air pressure is lower at the bottom of the mountain.

   B. It will contract because the air pressure is higher at the bottom of the mountain.

   C. It will become lighter. The air particles in the bottle weigh less because they are from the top of the mountain.

   D. It will not change because it is empty and contains no air.

At low elevations, air particles are packed together because the weight of the air above them is greater. At high elevations, there is less air above, so the particles are more spread out.

Wind

Air flows from high to low pressure. For example, air from an opened balloon will escape from the high air pressure inside the balloon to the lower air pressure outside the balloon. This movement of air is called *wind*. The greater the air pressure difference is between two places, the faster the air moves and the stronger the wind is.

7. Draw an arrow in the middle box to show which way the wind is blowing. Add the labels high pressure and low pressure on either side of the photo.

high

low

low

Air moves because of differences in air pressure.

Language SmArts
Describe Weather

8. Think back to the descriptions you wrote about the current weather, your favorite weather, and your least favorite weather. Choose one description and apply what you have learned to rewrite that description. Include the terms *temperature, humidity, precipitation, wind,* and *air pressure.*

   My favorite weather is snow. This weather has high humidity, lentempera high percipitation, low pressure and low wind speed

9. What might have caused the type of weather in your description? For example, why might it have been sunny, rainy, or windy?

   Rainy, in cold tempoature

Identifying Weather Associated with Pressure Systems

Air Pressure and Weather Maps

Air temperature varies because the sun warms Earth's surface unevenly. Because temperature affects pressure, differences in air temperature result in differences in air pressure. Differences in air pressure cause wind to blow. Wind moves clouds and precipitation from one place to another. On weather maps, an "H" shows where the air pressure is highest. An "L" shows where it is lowest. An *isobar* is a line that follows along points of equal air pressure. Observe the patterns in air pressure on the map.

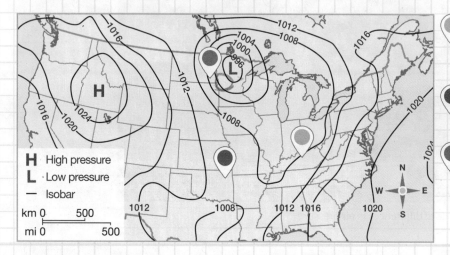

Each isobar traces along the same air pressure. The numbers show the measured air pressure in millibars (mb).

Where isobars are spaced far apart, the air pressure change is slight, so wind speed is lower.

Where isobars are spaced closely together, the air pressure change is great, so wind speed is higher.

Engineer It You are part of a committee that will choose a new location for a wind farm. In a wind farm, there are several wind turbines. Wind turbines generate power as wind turns their large blades. The higher the wind speed, the faster the blades turn and the more power the turbines can generate.

10. Apply what you know about air pressure, isobars, and wind speed. Mark an area on the map to show where you think the wind farm should be located.

11. The committee just learned that this map only shows conditions for one day. Is this enough information to tell if an area is normally windy? Are there any other criteria that would be important in deciding on the location of a wind farm? Write to the committee to explain your answers.

No. The map need to show the clima because weather usaally changes.

Pressure Systems

Examine the maps showing high- and low-pressure systems. A *high-pressure system* forms where air sinks toward the surface. As the air sinks, it spreads out from the high-pressure system toward areas of lower air pressure. Because Earth rotates, the air moves away from the high-pressure area in an outward spiral.

Where warm, less dense air rises from Earth's surface, a *low-pressure system* forms. This happens as air flows from higher-pressure areas toward a central area of low pressure and rises. The air moves into a low-pressure area as an inward spiral.

Pressure Systems and Weather

As air in a high-pressure systems sinks, it gets warmer. Relative humidity decreases, and if there were any clouds, they evaporate. These conditions usually bring clear skies and calm or gentle winds. In contrast, the air in a low-pressure system rises and cools. Clouds and rain form if the air rises and cools enough.

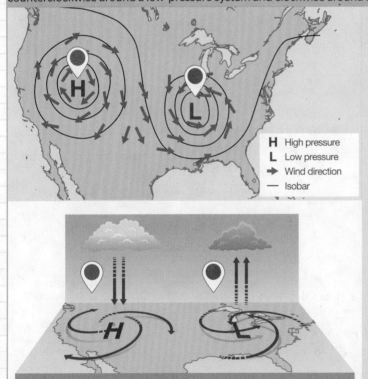

Air Pressure Systems in the Northern Hemisphere

Earth rotates, so wind does not blow in a straight line. In the Northern Hemisphere, air spirals counterclockwise around a low-pressure system and clockwise around a high-pressure system.

H High pressure
L Low pressure
→ Wind direction
— Isobar

High-pressure system Air sinks toward Earth's surface into an area of high pressure. Then the air spirals out toward areas of lower pressure.

Low-pressure system Air along the ground spirals inward toward an area of low pressure. Here, the air rises higher into the atmosphere and cools.

12. Write H or L to indicate whether each statement is associated with a high-pressure system or a low-pressure system in the Northern Hemisphere.

H	Sinking air becomes warmer
L	Rising air becomes cooler
H	Clear, sunny weather

L	Cloudy, rainy weather
H	Clockwise winds spread out
L	Counterclockwise winds move in

13. Think again about the storm that blew over the town in Utah. What kind of pressure system was probably involved? Record your evidence.

Interpret a Weather Map

A weather map shows the weather conditions of an area at a particular time. The map may include information such as temperature, humidity, wind, cloud cover, precipitation, and air pressure.

14. This map shows precipitation and air pressure. Label the map to describe the weather associated with each pressure system.

> Sunny and calm
> Rainy
> Snowstorms, windy

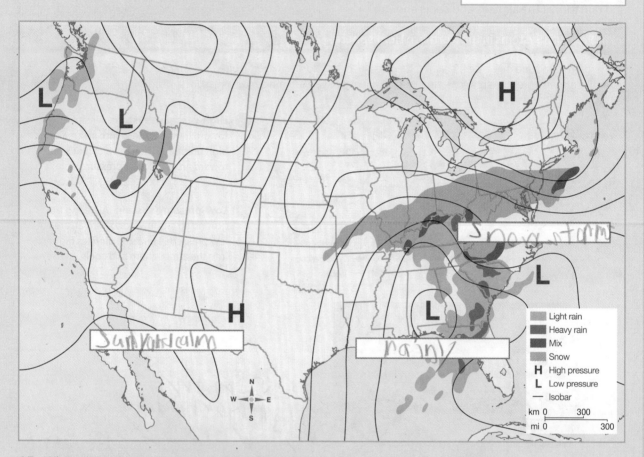

15. What patterns can you see in the map related to air-pressure systems and different weather conditions?

Low pressure zones have worse weather then high pressure.

Explaining How Fronts Change Weather

The Formation of Air Masses

An **air mass** is a large body of air that has similar temperature and humidity throughout it. An air mass develops over Earth's surface when air stays in one region for many days or weeks. The air mass gradually takes on the characteristics of the water or land below it. An air mass that forms above a warm, dry desert will be warm and dry. An air mass that forms above Arctic waters will be cool and humid.

16. What kind of air mass do you think forms over each region shown in the photos? Use the descriptions in the word bank to label each photo.

~~warm and dry~~
warm and humid
cool and dry
cool and humid

The Movement of Air Masses

Eventually, air masses move because of air pressure differences. As an air mass travels, it can slowly change as conditions on Earth's surface below the air mass change. When two different air masses meet, the warmer air mass will rise over the cooler air mass.

In the Gulf of Mexico, the water is warm. Therefore, warm and humid air masses form over the area. These air masses sometimes move toward land and run into cool and dry air masses. Think about what might happen as these two very different air masses collide.

(br) ©Robert Postma/Design Pics/Getty Images

Model an Air Mass Interaction

You will make a prediction about how a model will show the interaction between a warm and a cool air mass. You will then construct the model and use your observations to explain how warm and cool air masses interact.

MATERIALS
- container, shoebox-sized, clear, plastic
- food coloring, red
- ice cubes that contain blue food coloring
- water, warm

Procedure

STEP 1 The melted blue ice cubes represent a cold air mass, and the warm red water represents a warm air mass. Read through this procedure, and then use what you know about air masses to write a prediction about what might happen when the blue and red water interact.

STEP 2 Fill the plastic container half full of warm water. Let the water settle and become still.

STEP 3 On one side of the container, carefully place the blue ice cubes into the warm water.

Explore
ONLINE!

STEP 4 On the other side of the container, add a few drops of red food coloring.

STEP 5 Observe the interaction between the blue and red water. Record your observations.

Analysis

STEP 6 Was your prediction supported by your observations? Explain.

STEP 7 What type of weather might occur if these were two air masses interacting? Explain your thinking.

STEP 8 **Discuss** Is this a good model for showing how two air masses interact? Explain why or why not.

The Formation of Fronts

When two air masses of different temperatures and densities meet but do not mix, a front forms. A **front** is a boundary between air masses. The type of front that forms depends on the temperature, humidity, and motion of each air mass. The main types of fronts are cold fronts, warm fronts, stationary fronts, and occluded fronts.

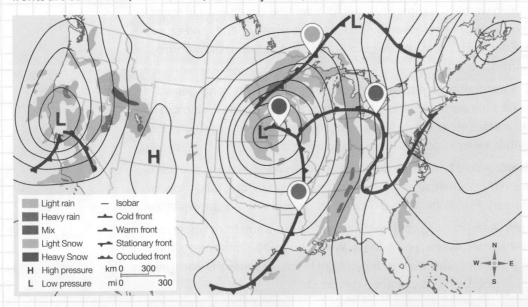

This weather map shows the air pressure, fronts, and precipitation on one day. Each type of front has its own symbol.

Light rain	— Isobar
Heavy rain	Cold front
Mix	Warm front
Light Snow	Stationary front
Heavy Snow	Occluded front
H High pressure	km 0 300
L Low pressure	mi 0 300

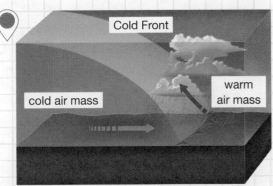

Cold Front

cold air mass | warm air mass

A **cold front** forms where a cold air mass moves under a warm air mass. This is shown by a blue line of triangles on the warm side that point in the direction that the front is moving.

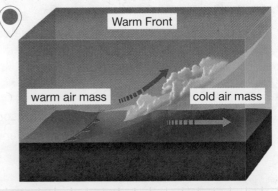

Warm Front

warm air mass | cold air mass

A **warm front** forms where a warm air mass catches up to and overrides a cold air mass. This is shown by a red line of half circles on the cold side that point in the direction that the front is moving.

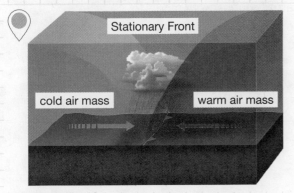

Stationary Front

cold air mass | warm air mass

A **stationary front** forms where a cold front slows down and stops as warm air moves toward it. This is represented by alternating blue triangles and red half circles.

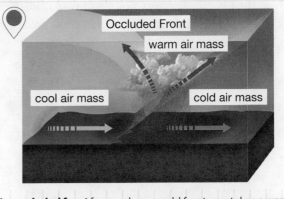

Occluded Front

warm air mass

cool air mass | cold air mass

An **occluded front** forms where a cold front overtakes a warm front. It is shown as purple alternating triangles and half circles headed in the direction the front is moving.

Fronts and Weather

Fronts commonly form as air masses rotate around low-pressure areas. As fronts move over places, they cause changes in temperature and precipitation. A front might also change wind speed and direction.

- **Cold front** A cold air mass wedges beneath a warm air mass, causing the warm air to rise. If the rising warm air is somewhat humid, scattered clouds form. If the rising warm air is very humid, the water vapor condenses into heavy clouds and causes precipitation. Cold fronts usually move quickly and can bring rain, snowstorms, and even thunderstorms.

- **Warm front** A warm air mass moves over a cold air mass. Warm fronts generally bring drizzly rain if the warm air mass is humid, or scattered clouds if it is more dry. Since warm air masses move slowly, the weather may remain rainy or cloudy for several days. After a warm front passes, warm weather is likely.

- **Stationary front** A cold front slows down and stops as warm air moves toward it. Water vapor in the warmer air mass rises and condenses to form rain, snow, or clouds. A stationary front generally causes many days of clouds and precipitation.

- **Occluded front** A fast-moving cold front catches up to a warm front where the warm air mass has risen over a cool air mass. When the cold air mass meets the cool air mass, a boundary called an occluded front forms. Because the warm air has been pushed up, clouds and precipitation can occur.

17. Fronts often form around areas of high /(low) pressure.

A sudden thunderstorm is most likely associated with the formation of a cold /(warm)/ stationary front.

EVIDENCE NOTEBOOK

18. Which type of front is most likely associated with the weather change in the town in Utah? Record your evidence.

Language SmArts
Compare and Contrast Information

19. In the experiment, you modeled a cold front. Compare and contrast your model to the other media in the lesson that show cold fronts. Compare their strengths and weaknesses.

_____

_____

_____

_____

_____

_____

_____

_____

Relating Earth System Interactions to Weather

Weather and the Earth System

The Earth system is made up of subsystems that work together:

- The *geosphere* is the mostly solid, rocky part of Earth.
- The *hydrosphere* is all of Earth's water.
- The *biosphere* is all living things on Earth.
- The *atmosphere* is the layer of air surrounding Earth.

Energy from the sun drives interactions among Earth's subsystems. These interactions affect weather patterns. Rocks, vegetation, and water on Earth's surface all absorb energy from the sun. For example, oceans absorb energy from the sun and the energy is exchanged with the atmosphere. This interaction causes coastal temperatures to vary less throughout the year than the temperatures of inland areas at the same latitude.

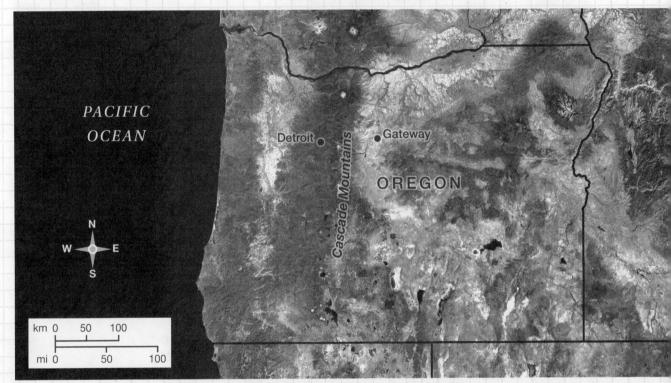

Detroit, Oregon, is at an elevation of about 0.5 km (1,595 ft) and has an average of 234 cm (91 in) of rain each year. Gateway, Oregon, is located at an elevation of about 0.56 km (1,791 ft) and gets about 25 cm (10 in) of rain per year.

20. Why do you think Gateway, Oregon, has very little rain throughout the year, whereas Detroit, Oregon, receives a lot of rain?

The Atmosphere and Weather

The intensity of sunlight is greater at the equator than at the poles. This results in temperature and air pressure differences across Earth. Along with Earth's rotation, air pressure differences result in global wind patterns and alternating belts of high and low air pressure at different latitudes. These global wind patterns are sometimes called *prevailing winds*. As the diagram shows, prevailing winds tend to move west to east over the United States and Canada. Prevailing winds influence weather because they affect the directions of moving air masses and fronts. They also drive ocean surface currents.

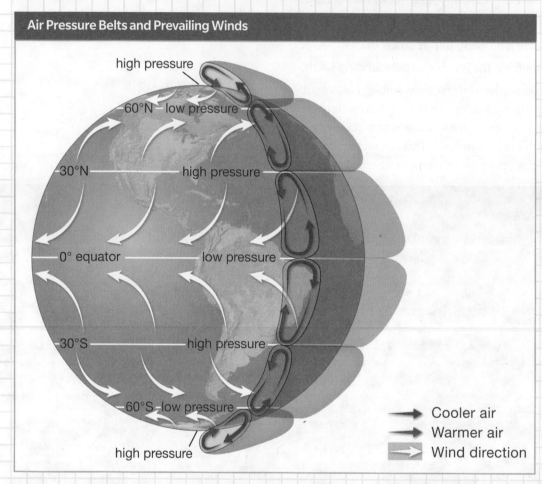

Air Pressure Belts and Prevailing Winds

high pressure
60°N low pressure
30°N
high pressure
0° equator
low pressure
30°S
high pressure
60°S low pressure
high pressure

→ Cooler air
→ Warmer air
⇒ Wind direction

21. Circle any statements that are true about pressure systems and prevailing winds.

    A. Air that has been heated at the equator forms a belt of low pressure.

    B. Air that has been heated at Earth's poles forms belts of low pressure.

    C. The uneven heating of Earth by the sun is the cause of pressure belts.

The Oceans and Weather

Prevailing winds move ocean water, forming surface currents. *Surface currents* occur at or near the ocean surface and flow around the globe. These currents redistribute the energy oceans absorb from the sun. Surface currents affect weather in coastal cities. For example, a warm ocean current called the North Atlantic Drift makes winters in western Europe warmer than one might expect at that latitude. Oceans also affect weather because humid air masses form over them and can bring rain to nearby areas.

Prevailing Winds and Surface Currents

The uneven heating of Earth's surface results in air pressure differences. This causes prevailing winds that influence the direction of ocean surface currents.

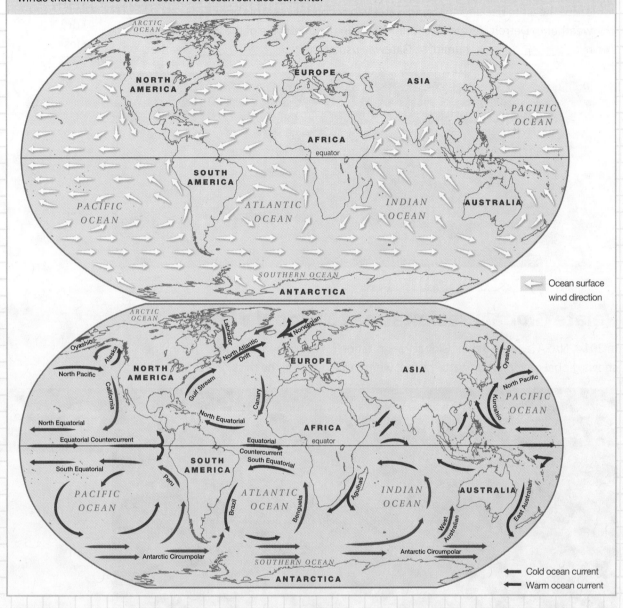

Ocean surface wind direction

Cold ocean current
Warm ocean current

22. Which phenomenon causes the other? Complete the statement to make it true.

Weather is affected by both prevailing winds and by surface currents that carry warm and cold ocean water around Earth. _____ cause _____.

WORD BANK
• Prevailing winds
• Surface currents

Landforms and Weather

Earth's landmasses affect weather in many ways. Both prevailing winds and ocean surface currents are redirected as they run into land. On land, there is a phenomenon known as the *rain shadow effect*. It occurs where prevailing winds bring humid air over mountains. As the humid air is forced to rise over the mountains, it cools and condenses into clouds and causes precipitation. Once the air reaches the other side of the mountain, it is drier. Therefore, one side of the mountain is cloudy and has more precipitation. On the other side, it is dry and the skies are often sunny.

23. Look back at the satellite image of Oregon. Using what you know about prevailing winds and the rain shadow effect, complete the description.

Prevailing winds bring humid air from the Pacific Ocean to Oregon. The mountains cause the air to rise and cool, and water vapor condenses. This brings _____ weather to Detroit. As the air continues down the other side of the mountain, it is _____ humid, so Gateway usually has _____ weather.

- rainy
- dry
- less

Relate Global Precipitation to Global Winds

In 2014, NASA launched their Global Precipitation Measurement mission. This image shows global precipitation patterns that were captured from the mission's satellite data.

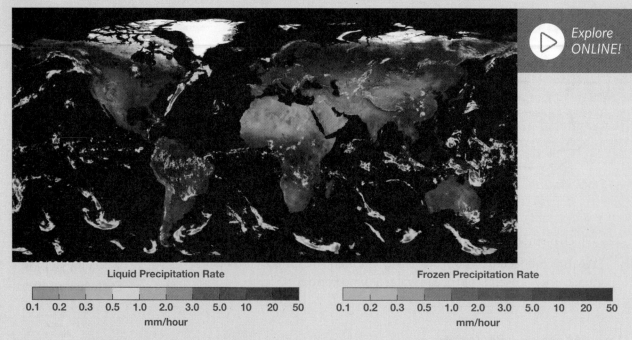

Explore ONLINE!

| Liquid Precipitation Rate |
| 0.1 0.2 0.3 0.5 1.0 2.0 3.0 5.0 10 20 50 |
| mm/hour |

| Frozen Precipitation Rate |
| 0.1 0.2 0.3 0.5 1.0 2.0 3.0 5.0 10 20 50 |
| mm/hour |

24. Apply what you have learned about weather and the Earth system to explain the patterns of precipitation on this satellite image.

_____
_____
_____
_____
_____

Continue Your Exploration

Name: Date:

Check out the path below or go online to choose one of the other paths shown.

Snowflake Sizes and Patterns

- **Hands-On Labs** ✋
- **El Niño and La Niña: Effects on Local Weather**
- **Propose Your Own Path**

Go online to choose one of these other paths.

Although snowflakes have a variety of structures, they are formed by the same process. As air temperature cools, tiny droplets of water freeze and form ice crystals. Many crystals have a symmetrical pattern with six "arms." As the crystals fall toward Earth, water vapor in the atmosphere freezes onto the crystals and they grow larger.

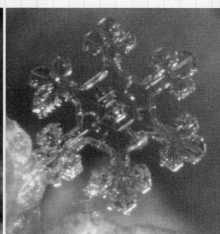

The unique shapes of individual snowflakes are a result of the temperatures in which they formed and fell to Earth. The six arms of the ice crystals have similar shapes because they all encountered the same conditions as the crystal fell through the atmosphere.

The Effects of Temperature and Humidity on Snowflakes

The variation in the shapes of snowflakes is a result of differences in air temperature and humidity. A crystal may begin to grow in one shape, but then as it falls through the atmosphere, changes in air temperature or humidity can cause it to grow in a different manner. For example, as air temperature increases during the snow crystal's descent, the sharper edges of a snowflake may become smoother.

The shape that the snow crystal has when it lands on a surface will determine the type of snow. Large snowflakes stack loosely on top of each other, leaving air pockets and producing fluffy, airy snow. Very cold temperatures and low humidity produce tiny snow crystals that can fall for hours and will barely build up. Warmer temperatures near freezing will produce heavy, wet snow.

Continue Your Exploration

The Effects of Temperature and Humidity on Snowflake Type

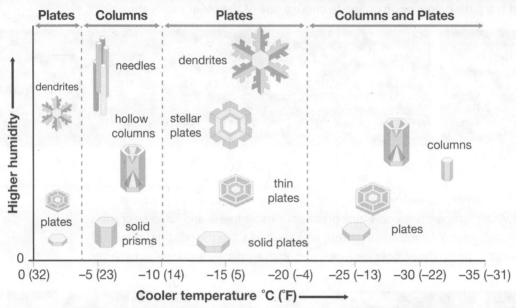

Credit: Adapted from "The physics of snow crystals, Figure 2, The snow crystal morphology diagram, doi:10.1088/0034-4885/68/4/R03" from *Reports on Progress in Physics*, Volume 68 by Kenneth G. Libbrecht. Copyright © 2012 IOP Publishing. Adapted and reproduced by permission of Kenneth G. Libbrecht and IOP Publishing Ltd.

1. What patterns do you notice in snowflake type and humidity across all temperatures?

2. Do the Math Over which temperature range do needles form? Tell whether these temperature ranges include positive or negative numbers.

Needles form between _____ °C and _____ °C, or _____ °F and _____ °F. Even though the Celsius temperature range includes _____ numbers and the Fahrenheit temperature range includes _____ numbers, they represent the same below-freezing temperatures.

3. What weather conditions might bring snow that is good for building a snowman? Explain.

4. Collaborate With a group, share your experiences with winter weather conditions. Have you ever seen snow? Have you noticed different types of snowfall? Discuss the factors that might have caused these different snow types.

Can You Explain It?

Name: _____   Date: _____

What could cause a storm like this to happen suddenly?

Explore ONLINE!

 EVIDENCE NOTEBOOK

Refer to the notes in your Evidence Notebook to help you construct an explanation for what causes sudden changes in weather like this storm.

1. State your claim. Make sure your claim fully explains how the storm suddenly occurred.

2. Summarize the evidence you have gathered to support your claim and explain your reasoning.

Checkpoints

Answer the following questions to check your understanding of the lesson.

Use the map to answer Questions 3 and 4.

3. What happens as energy from the sun warms Earth unevenly? Number the events 1–3 in the order of occurrence.

    _____ Global wind patterns form.

    _____ Temperature differences form across latitudes.

    _____ Air pressure differences form across latitudes.

4. Along 30° north and 30° south of the equator, air sinks along belts of high / low air pressure.

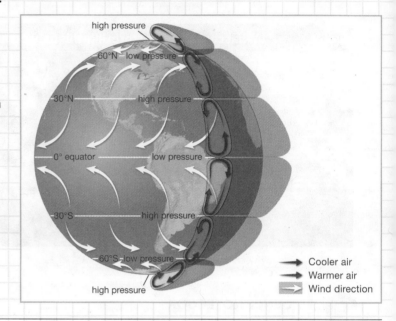

Use the map to answer Questions 5 and 6.

5. What type of weather do you notice near low-pressure areas?

    A. precipitation

    B. heat waves

    C. dry weather

6. What does the distance of the isobars near the high-pressure area tell you?

    A. They are close together, so it is windy.

    B. They are far apart, so it is windy.

    C. They are far apart, so winds are calm.

7. Which factors would most likely affect the weather on a small island in the ocean? Select all that apply.

    A. the formation of dry air masses

    B. ocean surface currents

    C. the formation of humid air masses

    D. isobars

8. Which is true about factors that influence weather?

    A. Precipitation type depends on air temperature.

    B. The rain shadow effect causes equal precipitation on both sides of a mountain.

    C. As air sinks, it absorbs moisture and forms rain clouds.

Interactive Review

Complete this section to review the main concepts of the lesson.

Temperature, humidity, and air pressure are factors that influence the weather we experience daily.

A. Explain how temperature and humidity are related and impact the weather.

High- and low-pressure systems affect the weather we experience.

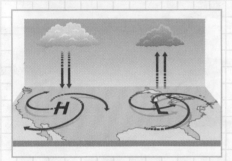

B. How do pressure systems affect the weather?

Air masses pick up characteristics over the regions where they form.

C. Provide an example of a front and explain how it forms.

Interactions among Earth's subsystems affect global weather patterns.

D. Choose two parts of the Earth system and give an example of how they interact to affect weather.

Weather Prediction

Weather prediction helps us prepare when we go outside.

By the end of this lesson . . .

you will be able to explain how weather predictions are made using mathematical models.

CAN YOU EXPLAIN IT?

How does this forecaster know that stormy weather is coming?

This weather forecaster uses weather maps and charts to show her prediction that a cold front is going to bring heavy rain and storms to the area over the next five days.

Explore ONLINE!

1. How might this forecaster predict future weather conditions? Describe any data or tools she might use and explain whether you think her prediction is accurate.

EVIDENCE NOTEBOOK As you explore this lesson, gather evidence to explain how weather predictions are made.

Using Mathematical Models to Make Predictions

Models in Science

How does an animal digest its food? Can a building withstand an earthquake? *Models* are tools that help scientists answer these kinds of difficult questions. Models are used in science to represent things that are large, small, dangerous, or complex. They help scientists make predictions and test ideas to find solutions to challenging questions.

It is possible for scientists to make models because events in nature often follow predictable patterns. For example, if you drop a ball from a certain height, you can predict how high it will bounce. Another pattern in nature is the yearly migration of some animals. Observing patterns in nature is the basis of science. These observations lead to explanations about the way the world works. Although these explanations are supported by observations, they may not be accurate. For example, the sun appears to move across the sky. For thousands of years, people observed this pattern and incorrectly concluded that Earth was the center of our solar system.

2. Describe the food web by writing *increase* or *decrease*.
   The rabbit population would _____ if the supply of grass became limited. This would happen because grass is a food source for rabbits. If the population of rabbits and mice decreased, the population of hawks would likely _____.

3. Write one question that the nautilus model could be used to answer. Write one question that the map could be used to answer.

This model is called a food web. It uses arrows to show eating relationships in an ecosystem. For example, rabbits eat grass and foxes eat rabbits.

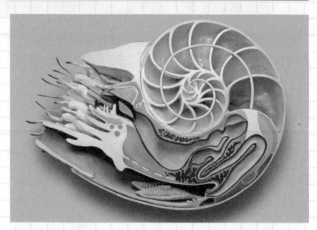

This model shows a cross-section of an animal called a nautilus. It has a shell made up of many chambers filled with gas to help the nautilus float. The nautilus fills its chambers with water when it wants to dive deeper.

This satellite image is a computer model that uses data about Earth. In the model, healthy vegetation stands out in red. Areas burned by wildfires are shown in black.

Mathematical Models

A *mathematical model* is a model that uses equations to represent the way a system or a process works. Some mathematical models are just a single equation. Others are more complex and involve many related equations. In order to use a mathematical model, data are collected. Next, data values are used to replace the variables of the equation or sets of equations in the model. Finally, calculations are made to get the results.

Mathematical Models and Prediction

Whether they are simple or complex, mathematical models can be used to make predictions. They can predict how something might work under different conditions. For example, you could use an equation to predict what an object would weigh on different planets. The equation is useful because we cannot easily travel to other planets and weigh the object. Mathematical models can also help to predict an event at a future time. Predictions can be shown on maps, graphs, and other displays.

 **Do the Math**
Predict Run Times Using a Model

Dwayne has been training for cross-country tryouts. He has been tracking his progress by recording his run times in a table every Saturday. Dwayne plotted his data on a graph. He decided to show the training week on the *x*-axis and his run times on the *y*-axis.

Dwayne's Weekly One-Mile Run Times	
Time (week)	Run Time (min)
Week 1	11.95
Week 2	12.25
Week 3	11.40
Week 4	10.10
Week 5	9.25
Week 6	8.60

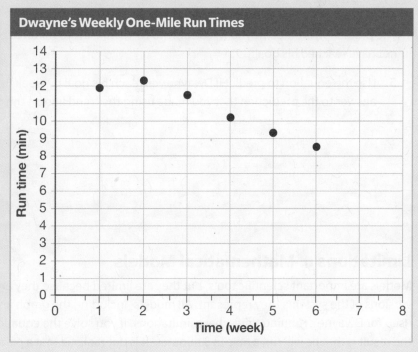

Dwayne's Weekly One-Mile Run Times

4. Dwayne's goal is to run 1 mile in 8 minutes or less. In order to predict when he will reach his goal, he drew a *trend line* that fits along the data points. Use a ruler to extend the trend line to week 8. According to the line, will he reach his goal by week 7? By week 8?

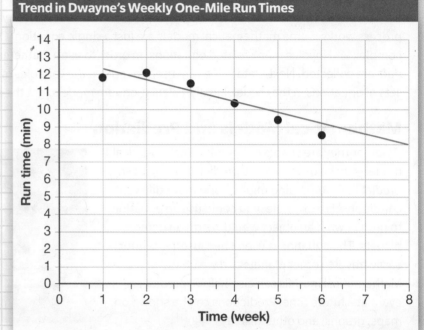

Trend in Dwayne's Weekly One-Mile Run Times

Did you know this line represents an equation? Another way to make a prediction about Dwayne's goal is to use the equation of the trend line:

$$y = -\frac{2}{3}x + 13$$

y = run time in minutes
x = time in weeks

The variable y represents Dwayne's run times. The variable x represents the week. To predict the run time for week 7, evaluate the equation for $x = 7$:

$$y = -\left(\frac{2}{3}\right)(7) + 13$$
$$y = 8.3 \text{ min}$$

The prediction is that Dwayne will be able to run a mile in 8.3 minutes by week 7. He will not have reached his goal.

5. Use the equation to predict if Dwayne will reach his goal by week 8. Compare your answer to the prediction that you made using the trend line on the graph.

Limitations of Mathematical Models

Models are important scientific tools, but they are limited because they are simplified versions of the systems they represent. All models, including the graph and equation used for Dwayne's running times, have limitations. If you solve the equation for week 15, the result is that he will run a mile in 3 minutes. It is not realistic that a person could run a mile in 3 minutes. Therefore, this model is only valid within a specific range of speeds.

Hands-On Lab
Predict Costs Using a Model

You will use a mathematical model to make predictions. Suppose you are a manufacturer who must ship rope of four different lengths to a store. You would like to figure out your shipping costs. For this, you need to know the weight of each piece of rope. However, you do not have time to weigh each piece. You can measure a few samples of rope and use a mathematical model to predict the weight of materials and estimate your costs.

MATERIALS
- meterstick
- rope, pieces of different lengths (4)
- spring scale with 5 g increments

Procedure and Analysis

STEP 1 Select four pieces of rope of different lengths.

STEP 2 Measure the length in centimeters of all four pieces of rope. Record your measurements in the table.

STEP 3 Measure the weight in grams of three individual pieces of rope. Record your measurements in the table. Set those pieces of rope aside.

	Rope 1	Rope 2	Rope 3	Rope 4
Length (cm)				
Weight (g)	actual:	actual:	actual:	predicted: actual:

STEP 4 Make a graph that plots the length and weight of the three pieces of rope. Include a title and be sure to label your x-axis and y-axis.

STEP 5 Use your graph to predict the weight of the fourth piece of rope. Record your prediction in the table.

STEP 6 Explain how you used your graph to predict the weight of the fourth piece of rope.

STEP 7 You need to ship 10 pieces of each length of rope. Estimate the total weight of the ropes you will be shipping.

STEP 8 How much would the shipment cost if the shipping rate was $1.00 per 1000 grams? Round to the nearest cent.

STEP 9 Measure the actual weight of the fourth piece of rope. Record your measurement in the table.

STEP 10 Compare your prediction to the actual weight of the fourth piece of rope. Was your prediction accurate? Can you explain why or why not?

STEP 11 Would your estimate for the shipping cost change when using the actual weight of the fourth piece of rope? Explain why your prediction was still useful even if it was not completely accurate.

STEP 12 **Engineer It** If you were a manufacturer, you would want your prediction to be as accurate as possible. Can you think of a way to improve your prediction?

Estimate Air Temperature with Cricket Chirps

Can crickets and a mathematical model help us estimate the temperature? Since the late 1800s, different equations have been developed to calculate the temperature based on the number of chirps a cricket makes over time. It was found that only certain species of crickets make reliable thermometers. The following equation works between 55–100 °F.

Snowy tree cricket chirp equation:
$T\,(°F) = N + 40$

Variables:

T = temperature (°F)

N = number of chirps every 13 seconds

This snowy tree cricket chirps at a different rate depending on the temperature outside! However, other things affect these crickets' chirp rates, such as age and mating behavior.

6. Do the Math Use the equation to calculate the temperatures in Limestone County and Socorro County. Write your answers in the last column of the table.

Location	Temperature Reading from Thermometer	N (chirps every 13 seconds)	T (calculated temperature)
Limestone County, Texas	76.6 °F	39	
Socorro County, New Mexico	54.5 °F	17	

7. What if you wanted to know how fast a cricket chirps at different temperatures? You would rearrange the equation to solve for N, which is the number of chirps:

$N = T - 40$

What is N if the temperature is 80 °F?

8. Think about the limitations of this model. Under what conditions is this cricket-chirping model accurate? Explain your answer.

_____

_____

_____

_____

Explaining the Accuracy of Weather Prediction

Weather Prediction

Have you ever seen a weather forecast online or in a newspaper? A **weather forecast** is a prediction about the state of the atmosphere at a given place and time. Weather forecasts are commonly provided using maps and weather charts. They can include predictions about temperature, wind, precipitation, cloud cover, and humidity. Have you ever used a weather forecast to make plans or decide what to wear? Weather forecasts not only help people plan their day, but they also provide warnings about severe weather such as blizzards and hurricanes. Pilots also rely on forecasts to navigate the planes we fly in. Who else might use weather forecasts?

9. This weather chart shows past and current temperatures. Try to predict the temperature for Friday.

Monday	Tuesday	Wednesday	Thursday (today)	Friday (tomorrow)
5 °F	0 °F	1 °F	−2 °F	

10. What did you base your prediction on? What other data would you want to use if you were asked to predict the weather?

11. Do you think your prediction would be within a degree of the actual temperature? Within three degrees? Within five degrees? Explain your answer.

Data Used in Weather Prediction

To make a weather forecast, past and current weather conditions are considered. This includes things such as wind speed, air pressure, humidity, cloud cover, precipitation, and temperature. Also taken into account are the current locations and movements of air masses, fronts, and high- and low-pressure systems.

Weather Forecast for Amarillo, Texas

	Wednesday Nov. 25	Thursday Nov. 26	Friday Nov. 27	
HIGH	**75 °F**	**60 °F**	**26 °F**	This row shows predictions for the high and low temperatures along with a description of the predicted weather for each day.
LOW	50 °F	22 °F	18 °F	
	Mostly Sunny	Scattered Thunderstorms	Freezing Rain and Windy	
	Chance of Precipitation 0%	Chance of Precipitation ⫽ 60%	Chance of Precipitation ⫽ 90%	**Precipitation** This is the predicted chance of precipitation.
	Wind ↗ southwest 14 mi/h	Wind ↑ south 16 mi/h	Wind ↙ northeast 20 mi/h	**Wind** Predicted wind speed is shown in miles per hour. Wind direction is shown with an arrow.
	Humidity 26%	Humidity 88%	Humidity 94%	**Humidity** This is the predicted relative humidity.

Weather Forecast Models

Past and current weather data are used to build weather forecast models. Weather forecast models are based on the physical laws that determine how the atmosphere works. Weather forecast models are mathematical models that are made up of many related equations. The equations represent the atmosphere and its interactions within the Earth system. Because so many factors influence weather, forecast models are very complex. For example, ocean currents affect humidity in some locations, and humidity impacts precipitation and cloud cover.

In the early 1900s, the first weather forecast model was used. It took so long to do the calculations by hand that, by the time the forecast was ready, the weather had already happened. By the 1950s, computers could do these calculations more quickly. Today, supercomputers do them even faster. Five-day forecasts can be made with about the same accuracy as a two-day forecast could thirty years ago. This is due to the continual improvement of weather forecast models and the speed of supercomputers. Many predictions are given as a chance or percentage for a general area because it is hard to predict exactly what will happen in an exact location. Meteorologists and forecasters analyze weather forecast model results before the results are shared with the public.

EVIDENCE NOTEBOOK

12. How do forecasters use mathematical models to make predictions about future weather conditions? Record your evidence.

Weather Forecast Maps for Nov. 25th – Nov. 27th

These weather forecast maps show predictions for precipitation, pressure systems, and fronts. Notice that Amarillo, Texas, is shown on these maps.

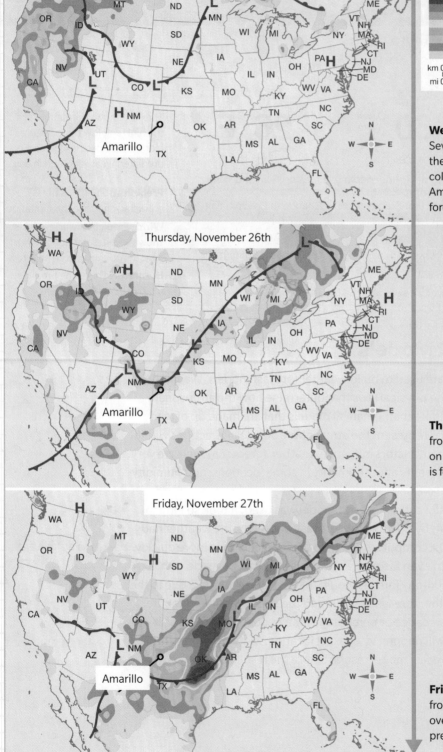

Precipitation Amount
Heavy precipitation
Light precipitation

H High pressure
L Low pressure
▼ Cold front
▲ Warm front
▼▲ Stationary front
▲▲ Occluded front

km 0   400
mi 0   400

Wednesday, November 25
Several fronts are moving through the United States. Notice the cold front moving south, toward Amarillo. No precipitation is forecast for Amarillo on Wednesday.

Thursday, November 26 The cold front is predicted to reach Amarillo on this day. Light precipitation is forecast.

Friday, November 27 The cold front is predicted to have moved over Amarillo by this day. Heavier precipitation is forecast.

13. Act With a partner, make a news forecast for the weather in Amarillo based on these maps. Be sure to describe the movement of the fronts and precipitation.

Limitations of Weather Forecast Models

All weather predictions contain some degree of uncertainty—that is, they are rarely 100% accurate. Weather is a complex phenomenon that is affected by many factors. One small change in a factor, such as wind direction or ocean circulation, can impact many other factors and result in different weather conditions. Because weather is complex, weather predictions are often given as a range or as a percentage of certainty. For example, you may see a forecast with a range of possible temperatures or the chance of rain given as a percentage.

Have you ever noticed a forecast that was wrong? Weather forecast models are constantly being improved. Predictions are compared to what actually happens with the weather. For example, if a forecast predicted the temperature on Friday, the actual temperature on Friday is compared to the prediction. This process would be followed for many days. If the predictions mostly match the recorded temperatures, then the model is a good predictor of temperature. If the model often predicts that it will be warmer or cooler than it actually is, then adjustments are made to improve the model. This process repeats as models are constantly improved to make predictions more accurate. Models are also improved in order to make predictions further into the future.

14. Look back to the forecast chart and maps for Amarillo. Compare these predictions to what actually happened with the weather. Describe your findings. If the forecast chart did not predict exactly what happened with the weather, explain why it is still useful.

Weather Observations in Amarillo, Texas

This weather chart shows past weather in Amarillo. These weather data were recorded for the same days the predictions were made.

Wednesday Nov. 25	Thursday Nov. 26	Friday Nov. 27
HIGH **76 °F**	**59 °F**	**29 °F**
LOW 35 °F	28 °F	22 °F
Mostly Sunny	Fog, Rain, and Snow Mix	Rain and Snow Mix
Precipitation Amount 0.00 in.	Precipitation Amount 0.52 in.	Precipitation Amount 0.34 in.
Wind ↗ southwest 15 mi/h	Wind ↑ south 17 mi/h	Wind ↙ northeast 21 mi/h
Humidity 48%	Humidity 90%	Humidity 90%

EVIDENCE NOTEBOOK

15. Why do weather forecast models have limitations? Why are they still useful to people? Record your evidence.

Analyze Weather Forecasts

Different models are used to predict weather for different ranges of time.

- Short-range weather forecasts make predictions for 0 to 3 days into the future.
- Medium-range weather forecasts make predictions for 3 to 7 days into the future.
- Long-range weather forecasts, or "outlooks," can range from weeks to months into the future.

In general, short-range forecasts are more accurate than forecasts made for longer periods of time. Given the continuous changes that occur in all of the factors that influence the weather, even short-range forecasts are not always 100% accurate.

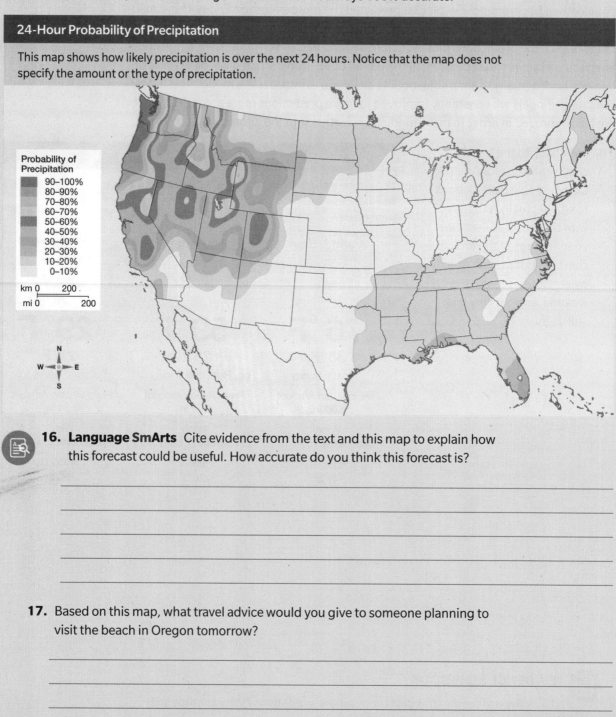

24-Hour Probability of Precipitation

This map shows how likely precipitation is over the next 24 hours. Notice that the map does not specify the amount or the type of precipitation.

16. **Language SmArts** Cite evidence from the text and this map to explain how this forecast could be useful. How accurate do you think this forecast is?

_____

_____

_____

_____

17. Based on this map, what travel advice would you give to someone planning to visit the beach in Oregon tomorrow?

_____

_____

_____

_____

Continue Your Exploration

Name: _____   Date: _____

Check out the path below or go online to choose one of the other paths shown.

People in Science

- **Hands-On Labs**
- **Hurricane Prediction**
- **Propose Your Own Path**

Go online to choose one of these other paths.

J. Marshall Shepherd, Meteorologist and Climatologist

Dr. Marshall Shepherd, who works at the University of Georgia, has been interested in weather since he made his own weather-collecting instruments for a school science project. Although the instruments he uses today, such as computers and satellites, are much larger and much more powerful than the instruments he made in school, they give him some of the same information.

In his work, Dr. Shepherd tries to understand weather events and relate them to current weather and climate change.

Do Cities Affect Rainfall?

Rainfall patterns are influenced by many factors, such as latitude, prevailing winds, and ocean currents. Some places are rainy because they are near an ocean or because they are located at certain latitudes. Other places are dry. For example, many deserts exist at 30 degrees latitude, both north and south of the equator. Dr. Shepherd and other scientists noticed increased rainfall in cities and in areas downwind of cities. For example, there was a 10-year thunderstorm study done in Atlanta, Georgia. The results, given in 2010, showed that during the summer months, there was an increase in rainfall and lightning over the city and downwind of the city, but not over the surrounding areas.

Continue Your Exploration

One explanation for the increased rainfall in cities is that dark surfaces, such as asphalt, absorb more energy from the sun than surfaces in a natural landscape do. Average temperatures in cities can be 6–8 °F (3–4 °C) warmer than the temperatures in natural landscapes surrounding a city. The warmer city surfaces warm the air directly above them. Because cities affect air temperature, they affect rainfall patterns. As warm air rises into the atmosphere, it begins to cool down. Moisture in the air forms clouds and brings rain to the city and to places downwind of the city, as seen in the Atlanta, Georgia, study. Another explanation is that cities can disrupt air flow because of the tall buildings. Just like air rises over a tall mountain and causes rainfall, city buildings may have the same effect.

1. One of the cities Dr. Shepherd has studied is Houston, Texas. He found that it rains more in Houston than in surrounding areas. What do you think will happen to rainfall amounts if Houston grows larger?

   A. Rainfall amounts will decrease in the city.

   B. Rainfall amounts will increase in the city.

   C. Rainfall amounts will be the same in the city.

2. **Draw** Make a diagram to show how cities might affect rainfall patterns. Include how a city's landscape impacts the flow of energy and the cycling of water.

3. A physical model is a miniature version of some part of the real world. How could you model how a city affects weather? Describe your physical model. What might you use to represent the sun, wind, rain, city surfaces, and natural surfaces?

4. **Collaborate** Research the historical weather data for a city that has grown very quickly over the past century. Are there any patterns in the precipitation data over time? Do you notice any other weather patterns that change over time? Record your observations. Share your results with a partner.

Can You Explain It?

Name: _____   Date: _____

How does this forecaster know that stormy weather is coming?

Explore
ONLINE!

EVIDENCE NOTEBOOK

Refer to the notes in your Evidence Notebook to help you construct an explanation about how weather predictions are made.

1. State your claim. Make sure your claim fully explains how this forecaster predicted the weather, including any data or tools she might have used. Describe the accuracy of her forecast.

2. Summarize the evidence you have gathered to support your claim and explain your reasoning.

Checkpoints

Answer the following questions to check your understanding of the lesson.

Use the graph to answer Questions 3–4.

3. Using a ruler, draw a single, straight trend line that comes as close as possible to all the points, and extend it to day 40. How tall will the seedling be on day 40 according to your trend line model?

   A. 42 cm

   B. 32 cm

   C. 38 cm

   D. 34 cm

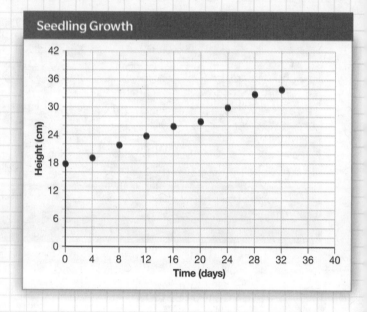

Seedling Growth

4. All models have limitations / graphs. By drawing a straight trend line on this graph, we are assuming the rate of growth is the same / changing. If the rate of growth changes as the plant ages, the line would / would not be straight and this model would not make a reliable prediction.

Use the map to answer Questions 5–6.

5. Currently, it is snowing in Fargo / Knoxville. It is likely to rain in Denver / Knoxville tomorrow because a cold / warm front is moving toward that area.

6. Rate the following predictions from 1 to 3, with 1 being the most accurate and 3 being the least accurate.

   _____ Tomorrow, it will be snowy in Fargo.

   _____ In seven days, it will be sunny in Denver.

   _____ In four days, it will be rainy in Knoxville.

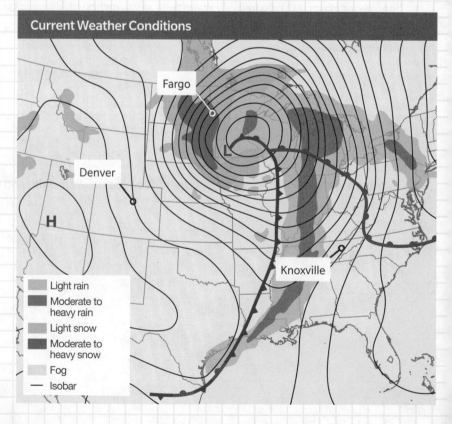

Current Weather Conditions

Light rain
Moderate to heavy rain
Light snow
Moderate to heavy snow
Fog
— Isobar

Interactive Review

Complete this section to review the main concepts of the lesson.

Mathematical models include equations that represent processes or phenomena. All mathematical models have limitations.

A. Why are mathematical models so valuable to scientists who study complex phenomena like weather?

Weather forecasts are made using mathematical models. These models include complex sets of equations that represent the many related factors that influence weather.

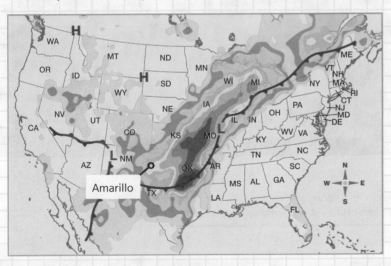

B. Weather forecast models have advantages and drawbacks. For example, one model may predict rain in a region with more accuracy than another model. Explain how the accuracy of a weather forecast model is tested.

Influences on Climate

The climate here brings snowy and cold winters. With little precipitation at other times of year, little vegetation grows.

By the end of this lesson . . .

you will be able to develop and use models to describe what factors influence regional climates in the Earth system.

CAN YOU EXPLAIN IT?

Why might these two regions in Asia have such different climates?

Taklamakan Desert

Singapore

equator

30°N

0°

30°S

INDIAN OCEAN

Taklamakan Desert China's largest desert has almost no vegetation. The average annual rainfall is around 1–2 cm (0.4–0.8 in.). Temperatures vary greatly, from –10 °C (14 °F) in January to 25 °C (77 °F) in July.

Singapore In the Singapore rain forest, the average temperatures remain fairly constant throughout the year—around 27 °C (81 °F). The high average annual rainfall of about 234 cm (92 in.) supports lush vegetation.

On the same day of the year, one person could be sweltering in the hot Singapore rain forest while another person is shivering on the edge of China's cold Taklamakan Desert.

1. What factors might cause the climates in Singapore and in the Taklamakan Desert to be so different from each other?

EVIDENCE NOTEBOOK As you explore the lesson, gather evidence to help explain why the climates in these two locations are so different.

Describing Climate

The world has many different climates. The average weather conditions in an area over a long period is called **climate**. Descriptions of climates usually include temperature and precipitation averages.

This area near Lake City, Colorado, is popular for ice climbing.

The Tottori Sand Dunes in Japan are perfect for sandboarding.

Cassis, France, attracts people from near and far for ocean adventures.

2. **Discuss** What types of weather are shown in the photos? Do the photos show what the weather is like all the time in each of these places?

Climate of San Francisco, California

This graph shows San Francisco's average monthly temperatures and precipitation totals. These averages were calculated over a long period of time, from 1981 to 2010.

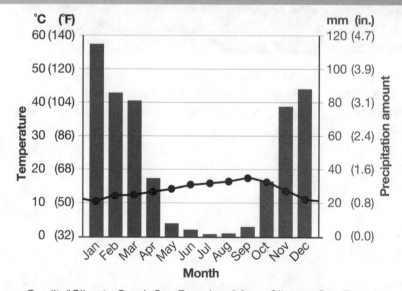

Credit: "Climate Graph San Francisco" from *Climate: San Francisco* by AM Online Projects. Copyright © AM Online Projects. Adapted and reproduced by permission of Alexander Merkel, AM Online Projects, © Climate-Data.org

Temperature The red line on the graph shows that the average temperature does not vary much over the year. It stays between 10 °C and 20 °C. It is coldest in January and warmest in September.

Precipitation Unlike temperature, the average precipitation amount varies greatly over the year. The blue bars show that the precipitation amount is highest from November to March and much lower from May to October.

Climate

Climate descriptions include the average temperatures and precipitation amounts over many years. Precipitation is usually expressed as average monthly totals. Average monthly temperature is also included in climate descriptions, and sometimes includes the average high and low temperatures for each month. Climate may also be described by how windy, cloudy, or humid a place is. Finally, an area's climate description can include its seasons—or its lack of seasons.

Climate graphs are used to display average monthly rainfall and temperature data. By comparing climate graphs from two different places, we can describe similarities and differences about their climates. Climate graphs also allow us to make predictions. For example, a climate graph could help a person predict the best time of year to plan an outdoor event.

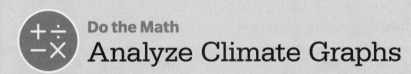

Do the Math
Analyze Climate Graphs

Imagine this: You won a trip to see the Great Wall of China, near the city of Beijing. To make sure that you can comfortably explore outside, you want to visit when the temperature is at or above 20 °C and when the chances of precipitation are low.

3. On the graph, circle the names of months with temperatures at or above 20 °C.

4. Of the months you circled, which month has the least amount of precipitation?

_____

5. The climate graph does not specify whether the precipitation is snow or rain. Use the graph to infer which time of year snow would fall and which time of year rain would fall. Explain.

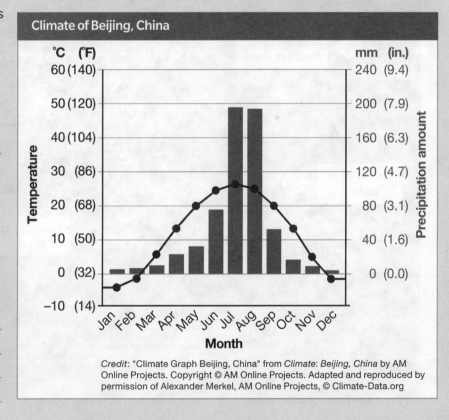

Credit: "Climate Graph Beijing, China" from *Climate: Beijing, China* by AM Online Projects. Copyright © AM Online Projects. Adapted and reproduced by permission of Alexander Merkel, AM Online Projects, © Climate-Data.org

Describing How Sunlight Affects Climate

Energy from the sun powers the Earth system and Earth's climate. The sun radiates energy. This energy travels in the form of waves and has to go about 150 million kilometers (93 million miles) through space before it reaches Earth. Look at the diagram. Energy enters the Earth system during the day when the sun is shining. Some of the energy is reflected and some is absorbed.

Earth's Energy Balance

Earth emits the energy it absorbs as radiation. This emitted energy drives currents in Earth's oceans and atmosphere and powers the climate system. Eventually, most of the energy emitted by Earth leaves the Earth system and goes back into space. So, the amount of energy coming into the Earth system roughly equals the amount going out.

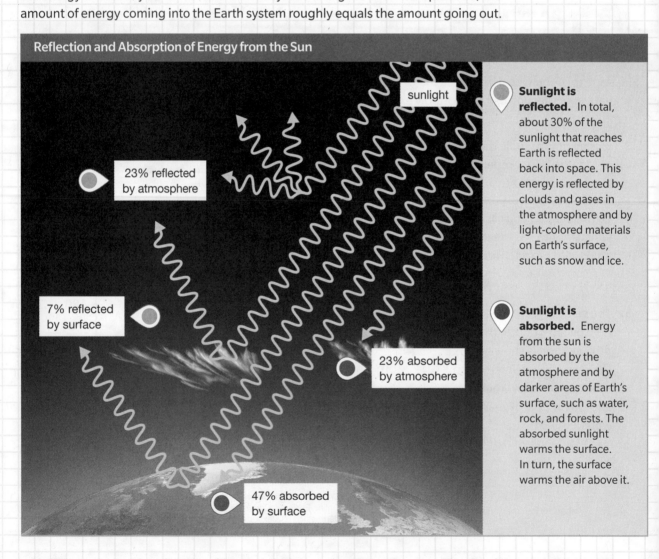

Reflection and Absorption of Energy from the Sun

sunlight

23% reflected by atmosphere

7% reflected by surface

23% absorbed by atmosphere

47% absorbed by surface

Sunlight is reflected. In total, about 30% of the sunlight that reaches Earth is reflected back into space. This energy is reflected by clouds and gases in the atmosphere and by light-colored materials on Earth's surface, such as snow and ice.

Sunlight is absorbed. Energy from the sun is absorbed by the atmosphere and by darker areas of Earth's surface, such as water, rock, and forests. The absorbed sunlight warms the surface. In turn, the surface warms the air above it.

Sunlight and Latitude

Latitude is the distance north or south of the equator. An area's climate depends on its latitude because latitude determines the intensity and amount of sunlight an area receives. Generally, the greater the intensity and the more sunlight received, the greater an area's temperature. Solar radiation arrives from the sun in essentially a straight line. However, because Earth's surface is curved, some of the sun's rays strike the surface more directly, while others strike at an angle.

6. **Collaborate** With a partner, model how sunlight strikes Earth. One person should shine a flashlight straight down onto a sheet of paper, and the other should trace the lighted area. Note the distance from the flashlight to the paper using a ruler. Next shine the flashlight on a different area of the paper at the same distance away, but tilt the flashlight at an angle. Trace this shape. Explain how this models the way sunlight strikes Earth. Can you think of a way to improve this model? Explain.

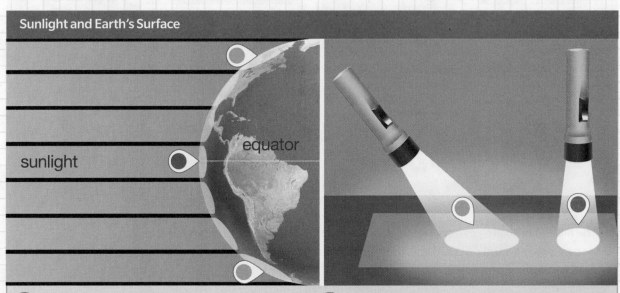

Sunlight and Earth's Surface

sunlight

equator

Near the equator, sunlight hits Earth most directly. Therefore, a certain amount of solar energy strikes a relatively small area. So, areas near the equator have higher temperatures than areas farther away from the equator do. When the flashlight is shined perpendicularly to the paper, the light strikes a relatively small area.

Near the poles, sunlight hits Earth indirectly. The same amount of sunlight is therefore spread over a larger area than at the equator. As a result, areas near the poles have lower temperatures than areas near the equator do. When the flashlight is shined at an angle, the light is spread over a larger area.

Albedos of Earth's Surface Materials

Different materials absorb and reflect different amounts of sunlight. *Albedo* describes how much sunlight a surface reflects. Generally, dark-colored surfaces absorb a lot of sunlight. That means dark surfaces do not reflect much sunlight and have low albedos. The absorbed energy warms the surfaces and the surfaces warm the air above them.

Light-colored surfaces generally reflect a lot of sunlight, so they have high albedos. Surfaces with high albedos stay somewhat cool because they reflect so much sunlight. Because these surfaces are cool, the air above these surfaces stays cool, too.

Albedo of Different Surface Types	
Surface	**Sunlight Reflected**
Fresh snow	80%–90%
Old snow	50%–60%
Ice	20%–45%
Beach, Desert	20%–40%
Grass	5%–25%
Soil	10%–15%
Forest	5%–10%
Water (sun near horizon)	50%–80%
Water (sun directly overhead)	5%–10%
Thick cloud	70%–85%
Thin cloud	25%–30%
Asphalt	5%–20%
Concrete	10%–35%

Albedo can be expressed as a percentage.

Mount Rainier National Park, Washington, in winter

Mount Rainier National Park, Washington, in summer

7. The albedo of an area can change with the seasons. During winter, snow reflects
~~more~~ / less sunlight than soil, rock, and vegetation that are exposed in summer do. Therefore, the albedo is higher / ~~lower~~ during winter.

EVIDENCE NOTEBOOK

8. Do you think the albedos of the surfaces in Singapore and the Taklamakan Desert affect their climates? Record your evidence.

Explain the Albedo Effect

Imagine an area covered in permanent snow and ice. The area has a high albedo, which means it reflects a lot of sunlight. If snow and ice start to melt, land is exposed and absorbs sunlight. Because land has a low albedo, the air above it warms, and more snow and ice melt. The *albedo effect* is a positive feedback cycle. Here is an example:

- An area has warmer-than-usual temperatures, so some ice and snow melt.
- Soil, rock, and vegetation are revealed, all of which have lower albedos.
- The soil, rock, and vegetation warm up as they absorb sunlight. In turn, they warm the air above them.
- The warmer air causes more ice and snow to melt, revealing more soil, rock, and vegetation. The cycle continues.

9. Draw Make a diagram to show how the albedo effect is a cycle that can cause changes to a snow-covered area. You can refer to the text or table for information.

10. Engineer It You are part of a planning group that is developing a city park. You want to keep the amount of sunlight absorbed at a minimum. Based on what you have learned about the albedo of different surfaces, write a recommendation for a plan to help the group achieve their goal.

_____

_____

_____

_____

_____

_____

Explaining What Influences Climate

Factors That Influence Climate

Around the world, different climates exist, from hot to cold and from dry to rainy. Factors in the Earth system that influence climate include prevailing winds, ocean currents, large bodies of water, and landforms. Latitude and elevation also affect climates.

11. Compare today's weather with your area's climate. What do you think caused the weather today? Might those factors be similar to factors that determine the climate?

Latitude

The intensity of the sunlight is greater at the equator than at the poles, so the temperature is higher at the equator than at the poles. Look at the diagram. These temperature differences cause air pressure differences. Along with Earth's rotation, these pressure differences result in global wind patterns and alternating belts of high and low air pressure at different latitudes. Near the equator, warm, moist air rises and cools, and water vapor condenses to form clouds and rain. Therefore, rainy climates commonly exist near the equator. A similar process occurs near 60°N and 60°S, causing rainy climates in those regions. In contrast, cool, dry air sinks along high-pressure belts near 30°N and 30°S and at the poles. These areas commonly have dry climates.

Explore ONLINE!

Latitude's Effect on Climate Patterns

The intensity of sunlight at different latitudes results in different climates.

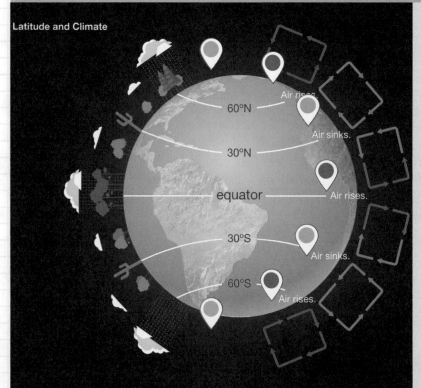

Latitude and Climate

60°N — Air rises.
Air sinks.
30°N
equator — Air rises.
30°S
Air sinks.
60°S — Air rises.

Around low-pressure belts, air rises, cools, and forms clouds and precipitation. Low-pressure belts result in wet climates.

Around high-pressure belts, air sinks and dries, resulting in clear skies and little precipitation. High-pressure belts correspond to dry climates.

Prevailing Winds

Prevailing winds are global patterns of wind that generally move in a certain direction. Prevailing winds affect climate because they move air masses from one place to another. For example, cool, moist air masses that form over the Pacific Ocean are carried to the northwest coast of the United States by prevailing winds. Prevailing winds also drive ocean surface currents that travel the globe and constantly move both warm and cool ocean water.

12. Use the terms in the word bank to complete the table to summarize patterns in air pressure, temperature, and precipitation at different latitudes.

WORD BANK	
• high	• warm
• low	• dry
• coolest	• wet

Latitude	Air Pressure	Temperature	Precipitation
Poles	high		dry
60°N and 60°S	low	cool	
30°N and 30°S			
Equator		warmest	wet

Ocean Currents

Ocean currents move water and distribute energy and nutrients around the globe. *Surface currents* are driven by prevailing winds. They carry warm water away from the equator and cool water away from the poles. Currents moderate coastal cities' temperatures as cold currents cool warmer air and warm currents warm cooler air. For example, the waters of the Gulf Stream move warm water from the Gulf of Mexico northeastward toward Great Britain. The British climate is mild in part because of the warm Gulf Stream and the North Atlantic Drift.

Elevation

Elevation also influences climate. *Elevation* is a place's distance above sea level. As elevation increases, air temperature decreases. It is usually cooler at higher elevations and warmer at lower elevations. So, the air feels colder as hikers climb higher up a mountain. Imagine cities at the same latitude and far from a large body of water. These cities can have very different climates if they are at different elevations.

 EVIDENCE NOTEBOOK

13. Think about Singapore and the Taklamakan Desert as you continue to explore this section. What factors might influence their climates? Record your evidence.

Large Bodies of Water

Different surfaces release energy at different rates. For example, water absorbs and releases energy more slowly than land does. As a result, oceans keep the temperature of nearby land from changing as much as it would if there was no water nearby. Therefore, the temperatures of coastal areas do not tend to vary as greatly as areas that are farther inland along similar latitudes. Nearby bodies of water increase the amount of water in the air. Because of this, places near large bodies of water often receive more precipitation than they would if the body of water were not present.

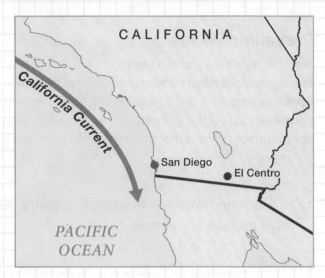

14. The average annual high temperature in El Centro varies from about 15 °C to 31 °C. In San Diego, it only varies from about 14 °C to 21 °C. The more moderate temperatures in San Diego / El Centro are due to its nearness to the ocean. A cold ocean current also affects the climate of San Diego / El Centro.

Landforms

Landforms such as tall mountains can create very different climates on each side of the mountain. In some places, prevailing winds move moist air toward mountains. As the moist air rises to pass over the mountain, it cools and condenses into clouds and precipitation. Rain or snow falls on the side of the mountain where the prevailing winds are coming from. The air that reaches the other side of the mountain is drier, so very little precipitation occurs. This side is said to be in a *rain shadow*.

15. Draw an arrow to show the direction of prevailing winds. Label the diagram to show which side has a rainy climate and which side has a dry climate.

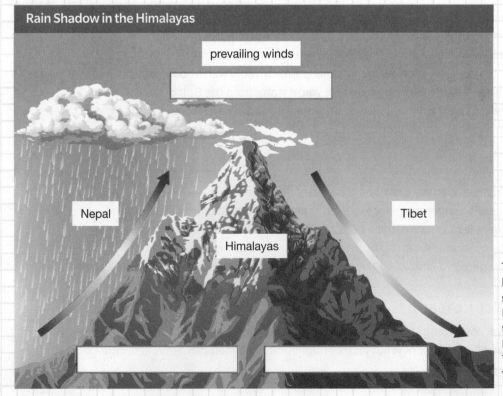

The Tibetan Plateau lies in the rain shadow of the Himalayas. In fact, the Taklamakan Desert is part of the Tibetan Plateau.

Compare Climates

Phoenix and Flagstaff are two cities in Arizona. Look at the map. These cities are only 233 km (145 mi) apart. However, their climates are different from one another, especially during winter.

Climate of Flagstaff, Arizona

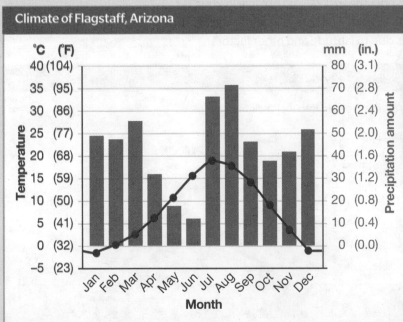

- Elevation: 2,106 m (6,909 ft)
- Average annual temperature: 6.6 °C (43.8 °F)
- Average annual precipitation: 588 mm (23 in.)

Credit: "Climate Graph Flagstaff, Arizona" from *Climate: Flagstaff, Arizona* by AM Online Projects. Copyright © AM Online Projects. Adapted and reproduced by permission of Alexander Merkel, AM Online Projects, © Climate-Data.org

Climate of Phoenix, Arizona

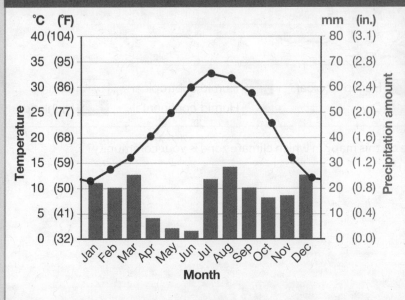

- Elevation: 328 m (1,076 ft)
- Average annual temperature: 21.5 °C (70.7 °F)
- Average annual precipitation: 211 mm (8 in.)

Credit: "Antananarivo Climate Data" from *Climate: Antananarivo* by AM Online Projects. Copyright © AM Online Projects. Adapted and reproduced by permission of Alexander Merkel, AM Online Projects, © Climate-Data.org

16. Use the data to explain why the climates of these cities are different in the winter.

_____

_____

_____

Using Regional Climate Models

Earth's Major Climate Zones

Frogs do not live at the North Pole, and polar bears likely do not live in your neighborhood. This has to do with Earth's climate zones. Each zone has different temperature and precipitation patterns due to latitude and other factors.

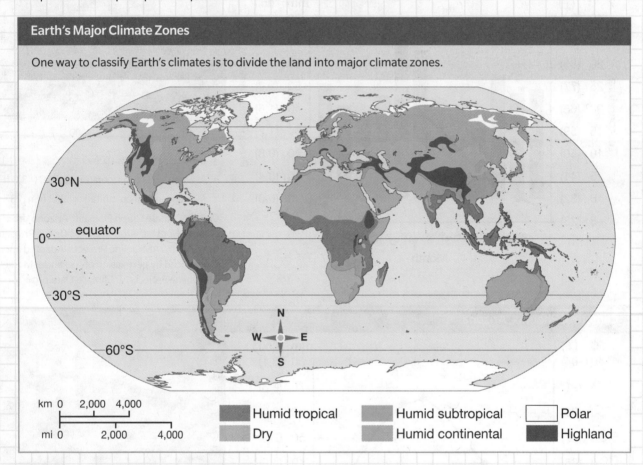

Earth's Major Climate Zones

One way to classify Earth's climates is to divide the land into major climate zones.

17. Are you able to find where you live on this map? In which climate zone is your community?

Earth's Regional Climates

It can be helpful to define the major climate zones, but there are actually many more regional climates within these zones. These more specific regional climates result from climate influences such as landforms, elevation, and ocean currents.

Hands-On Lab
Model Your Climate

You will develop and use a model to describe your local climate. You will use the model as a visual display in a multimedia presentation to explain the factors that influence your local climate.

MATERIALS
• Materials for climate models will vary.

Procedure and Analysis

STEP 1 Define your area of study. This might be the city you live in or a region.

STEP 2 Gather climate data for your area. Summarize the climate, including temperature and precipitation patterns. Note if there are seasons or winds, and how much and what kind of precipitation falls throughout the year.

STEP 3 Describe what factors influence your climate, or what your model's "inputs" will be. Think about latitude, elevation, surface type, prevailing winds, landforms, and ocean currents.

STEP 4 Plan a way to model your climate. How will your model show the inputs in your local climate system?

STEP 5 How will your model show the outputs in your local climate system? For example, how will it represent temperature and precipitation patterns?

STEP 6 Identify the materials you will need to make your model.

STEP 7 Check in with a teacher to describe your plans and materials needed. Get confirmation that you are ready to proceed. Then develop your model.

STEP 8 **Language SmArts** Make a multimedia presentation to help clarify your model and emphasize your main points. Present this to the class.

Earth's Regional Climates

Within each major climate zone are smaller regional climates. Explore the map and photos.

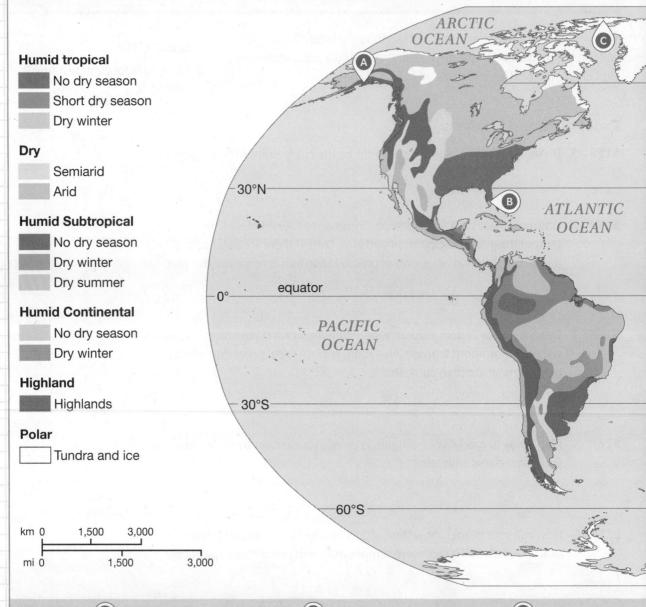

Humid tropical

No dry season
Short dry season
Dry winter

Dry

Semiarid
Arid

Humid Subtropical

No dry season
Dry winter
Dry summer

Humid Continental

No dry season
Dry winter

Highland

Highlands

Polar

Tundra and ice

km 0   1,500   3,000

mi 0   1,500   3,000

ARCTIC OCEAN

ATLANTIC OCEAN

30°N

equator

0°

PACIFIC OCEAN

30°S

60°S

Anchorage, Alaska, has short, cool summers and snowy winters. Temperatures are milder here than inland cities at similar latitudes because it is near the ocean.

This swamp in southern Florida is located in the only tropical climate zone in the continental United States.

The arctic hares of Ellesmere Island, Canada, thrive in the polar climate of the area with its long, cold winters and brief, cool summers.

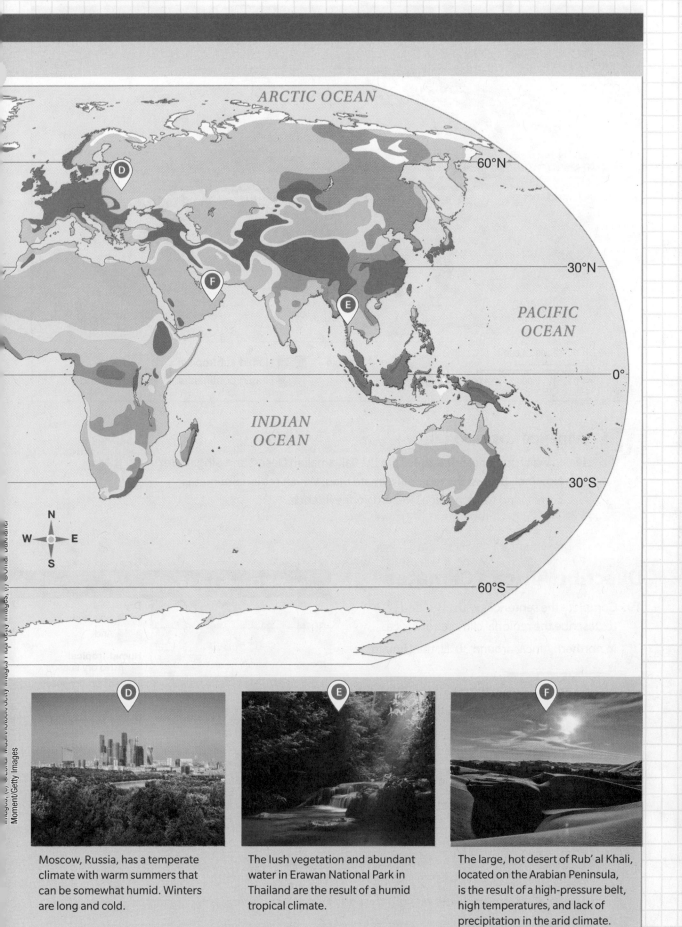

ARCTIC OCEAN

60°N

30°N

PACIFIC
OCEAN

0°

INDIAN
OCEAN

30°S

60°S

N
W   E
S

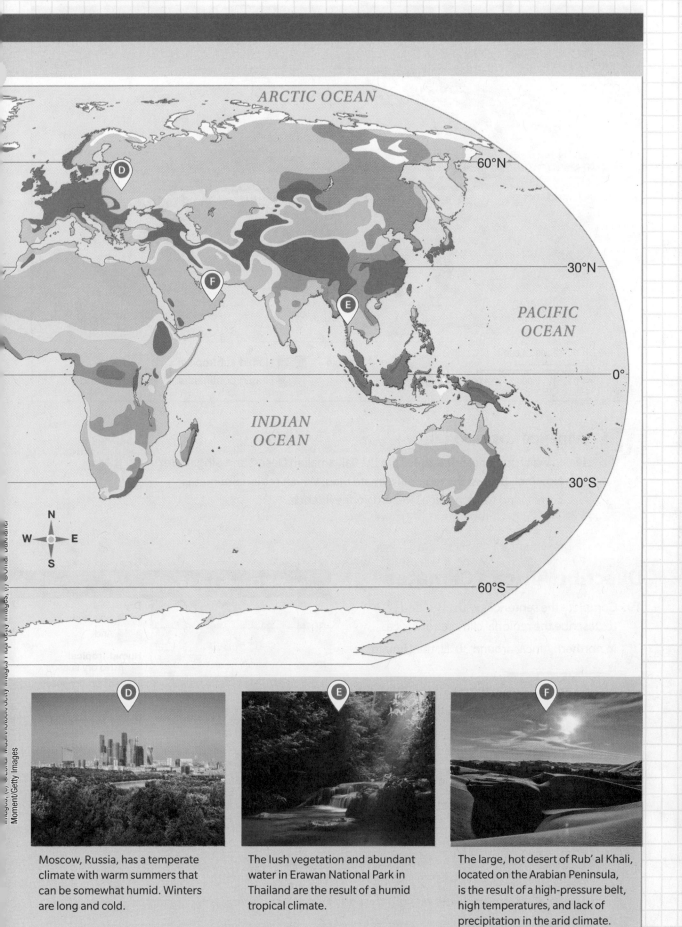

D Moscow, Russia, has a temperate climate with warm summers that can be somewhat humid. Winters are long and cold.

E The lush vegetation and abundant water in Erawan National Park in Thailand are the result of a humid tropical climate.

F The large, hot desert of Rub' al Khali, located on the Arabian Peninsula, is the result of a high-pressure belt, high temperatures, and lack of precipitation in the arid climate.

Earth's Major Climate Zones

Revisit the major climate zones on Earth.

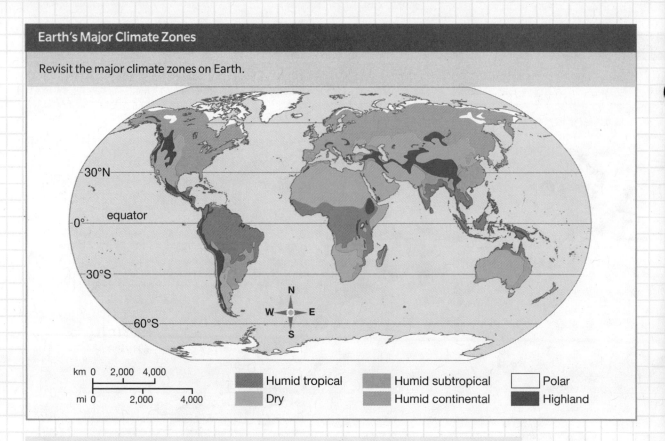

▮ Humid tropical		▮ Humid subtropical		▯ Polar	
▮ Dry		▮ Humid continental		▮ Highland	

 EVIDENCE NOTEBOOK

18. In which major climate zones are the Taklamakan Desert and Singapore? Now look back at the regional climate map. Which regional climates correspond to each place? Record your evidence.

Describe Africa's Climates

19. Complete the sentences with dry and humid to describe the regional climates of Africa.

   In northern Africa, around 30°N, the climate is _____.

   Around the equator, in the middle of Africa, the climate is _____.
   Around 30°S, the climate is mostly _____.

20. **Discuss** Do you think elevation affects the climate in Africa? Explain your answer.

   _____

   _____

   _____

   _____

   _____

   _____

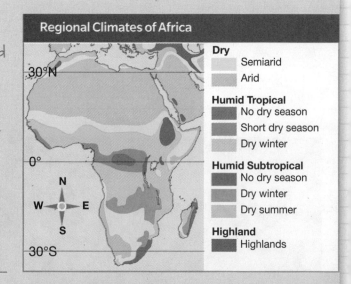

Regional Climates of Africa

Dry
▮ Semiarid
▮ Arid

Humid Tropical
▮ No dry season
▮ Short dry season
▮ Dry winter

Humid Subtropical
▮ No dry season
▮ Dry winter
▮ Dry summer

Highland
▮ Highlands

Continue Your Exploration

Name: _____   **Date:** _____

Check out the path below or go online to choose one of the other paths shown.

> **Exploring the Greenhouse Effect**

- **Hands-On Labs** ✋
- **Lake Effect**
- **Propose Your Own Path**

Go online to choose one of these other paths.

The Greenhouse Effect

How does a greenhouse work? Sunlight passes through the glass and warms the floor and objects inside. In turn, the air inside the greenhouse warms. The warm air is trapped by the glass, so the interior of the greenhouse gets warmer.

The windows in a greenhouse are similar to Earth's atmosphere. Sunlight passes through the atmosphere and warms the surface. This causes the air to warm. Some of the energy is absorbed by *greenhouse gases* in the atmosphere. This phenomenon, called the *greenhouse effect,* is what makes Earth warm enough for humans and many other plants and animals to live. However, human activities have rapidly increased the amount of greenhouse gases in the past few hundred years. This increase has caused Earth's average global temperature to rise. Rising temperatures have some negative impacts on the environment, which we depend on for water, food, and other resources.

Greenhouse Gases

Naturally occurring greenhouse gases include water vapor, carbon dioxide, methane, nitrous oxide, and ozone. Human activities have caused their levels to rise. Chlorofluorocarbons (CFCs) are human-made greenhouse gases that come from using refrigerants, aerosols, and cleaning solvents.

Gases in the atmosphere retain heat, which is similar to the way a greenhouse retains heat.

Getty Images

Continue Your Exploration

Common Greenhouse Gases and Their Sources

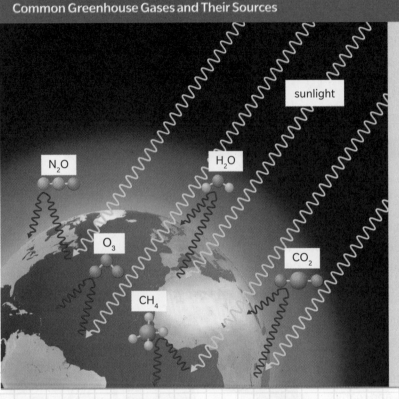

sunlight

N$_2$O

H$_2$O

O$_3$

CO$_2$

CH$_4$

Carbon dioxide (CO$_2$) occurs naturally in the atmosphere, but humans have increased levels by burning coal, oil, natural gas, and wood.

Nitrous oxide (N$_2$O) is naturally present in the atmosphere, but human use of fertilizers in agriculture and burning fossil fuels is increasing the amount.

Water vapor (H$_2$O) occurs naturally in the atmosphere and is the most abundant of the greenhouse gases. The amount of water vapor has increased with increasing global temperatures.

Methane (CH$_4$) occurs naturally in the atmosphere, but humans have increased amounts due to oil and gas production, raising cattle, and producing garbage.

Ozone (O$_3$) occurs naturally in the atmosphere but can also be produced by automobile exhaust, pollution from factories, and burning vegetation.

1. Write the correct term from the word bank to complete the paragraph. You may use a term more than once.

   As greenhouse gases have _____, the global average temperature has _____. Warmer global temperatures have _____ sea ice and caused sea levels to rise.

   WORD BANK
   • increased
   • decreased

2. Make an X next to the actions that would increase levels of greenhouse gases.

   _____ driving a car that burns fossil fuels

   _____ riding a bike and walking

   _____ using fertilizer to grow crops

   _____ eating less meat from cattle

3. Why do you think humans continue to do the activities that increase greenhouse gases in the atmosphere?

4. **Collaborate** Work with classmates to develop a plan for your school to reduce the amount of greenhouse gases it produces. In your plan, include inputs and outputs related to the greenhouse effect. You may want to use a sketch or diagram to describe your plan. Share your plan with your class.

Can You Explain It?

Name: **Date:**

Why might these two regions in Asia have such different climates?

Singapore

Taklamakan Desert

EVIDENCE NOTEBOOK

Refer to the notes in your Evidence Notebook to help you construct an explanation for the differences between the climates of the two locations.

1. State your claim. Make sure your claim fully explains why the climates of the two locations are so different.

2. Summarize the evidence you have gathered to support your claim and explain your reasoning.

Checkpoints

Answer the following questions to check your understanding of the lesson.

Use the graph to answer Questions 3 and 4.

3. The graph shows the average annual temperatures of four cities, which were calculated from 30 years of data. This graph therefore helps to describe each area's weather / climate.

4. Look at the latitude of each city. Select all that apply. On average:

   A. The cities at higher latitudes have less precipitation.

   B. The cities at lower latitudes are colder.

   C. The cities at lower latitudes are warmer.

   D. The cities at higher latitudes have a greater range in temperatures over the year.

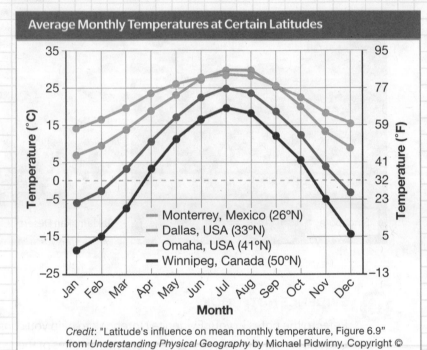

Average Monthly Temperatures at Certain Latitudes

— Monterrey, Mexico (26°N)
— Dallas, USA (33°N)
— Omaha, USA (41°N)
— Winnipeg, Canada (50°N)

Credit: "Latitude's influence on mean monthly temperature, Figure 6.9" from *Understanding Physical Geography* by Michael Pidwirny. Copyright © 2014-2017 Our Planet Earth Publishing. Adapted and reproduced by permission of Our Planet Earth Publishing.

5. Tobias modeled the albedo effect by laying large white and black T-shirts out in the sun. He measured the temperature / precipitation of each shirt for a few hours. The end result was that the white / black shirt was warmer.

Use the map to answer Question 6.

6. What explains the different climates of London and Natashquan?

   A. different latitudes

   B. distance from the ocean

   C. different ocean currents

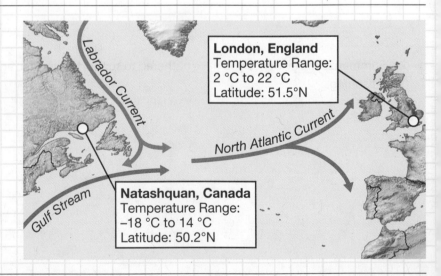

London, England
Temperature Range:
2 °C to 22 °C
Latitude: 51.5°N

Natashquan, Canada
Temperature Range:
−18 °C to 14 °C
Latitude: 50.2°N

Labrador Current

North Atlantic Current

Gulf Stream

7. Snow reflects / absorbs more sunlight than water does. Snow has a lower / higher albedo than water. As snow melts, more / less sunlight is absorbed by the darker soil beneath it. This causes cooling / warming.

Interactive Review

Complete this section to review the main concepts of the lesson.

An area's climate is described by its average temperature and precipitation patterns over a long period of time.

A. Why does describing an area's climate require weather data for more than one or two years?

Areas near the equator receive more direct sunlight than areas near the poles.

B. How is climate affected by latitude?

Factors that influence climate include latitude, prevailing winds, ocean currents, elevation, surface type, and landforms.

C. Provide an example of how two or more climate factors are related.

Earth's major climate zones can be divided into smaller regional climates.

D. Explain why climates zones and regional climates do not follow latitude lines exactly.

Choose one of the activities to explore how this unit connects to other topics.

☐ Physical Science Connection

High-Altitude Weather Balloons Scientists launch weather balloons with sensors attached to gather data about current atmospheric conditions and to predict future weather.

Using library or Internet resources, research high-altitude balloons to determine how weather balloons reach high altitudes without engines and why scientists use them. Then make a multimedia presentation to share what you learned with your class.

☐ Engineering Connection

Building Homes for Different Climates Architects design houses that shelter and protect people from particular environmental conditions. To design homes that are suitable for various climates, architects must understand the unique characteristics of each region's climate. They must also understand the types of building materials that are available and sustainable in that environment.

Research home designs and building materials architects use in different climates and locations. Create a visual display explaining the vast range of materials available to construct homes in various climates and locations.

☐ Social Studies Connection

Alaskan Inuit Culture The native Alaskan Inuit people inhabit the West, Southwest, far North, and Northwest parts of Alaska. They were one of the last native groups to come to North America. In Alaska, the average daytime winter temperature is generally below freezing. The local weather and climate have a great impact on Inuit culture.

Research the Alaskan Inuit people to determine how they have adapted their way of living to such a cold climate. Create a multimedia presentation that includes how the local weather patterns affect the clothing, housing, transportation, and other lifestyle factors of the Inuit people.

Name: _____   Date: _____

Complete this review to check your understanding of the unit.
Use the map showing the isobars to answer Questions 1 and 2.

1. Which point on the map is the windiest right now?

   A. Point A

   B. Point B

   C. Point C

   D. Point D

2. The fronts on this map are moving in a clockwise / counterclockwise direction. A warm front will likely pass through point A / B in the near future.

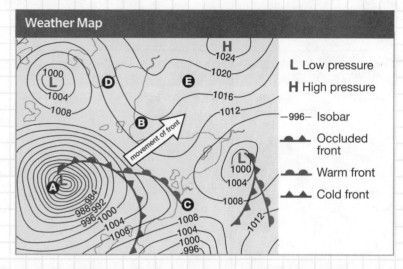

Weather Map

L Low pressure
H High pressure
—996— Isobar
Occluded front
Warm front
Cold front

Use the map to answer Questions 3 and 4.

3. This weather / climate map shows the average type / amount of precipitation in Colorado during the year.

4. Which of the following factors could cause the precipitation average in Vail to be higher than the precipitation average in Monte Vista?

   A. Vail is in a different county.

   B. Monte Vista is in a rain shadow.

   C. The temperature is usually hotter in Monte Vista.

   D. Monte Vista is south of Vail.

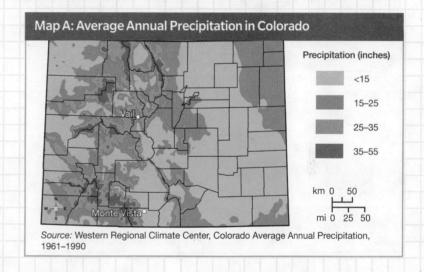

Map A: Average Annual Precipitation in Colorado

Precipitation (inches)
<15
15–25
25–35
35–55

km 0   50
mi 0 25 50

Source: Western Regional Climate Center, Colorado Average Annual Precipitation, 1961–1990

6. Complete the table by providing examples of how the factors that influence weather and climate relate to each big concept.

Factors that Influence Weather and Climate	Cause and Effect	System Interactions	System Models
Global Winds	Global winds are caused by the uneven heating of Earth's surface and the rotation of Earth.		
Ocean Currents			
High and Low Air Pressure			

Name: _____   Date: _____

Use the map to answer Questions 7–9.

Ocean Currents between Atlanta and Casablanca

The map shows two cities at the same latitude—Atlanta in the United States and Casablanca in Morocco.

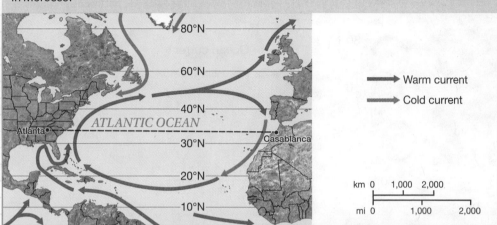

7. Atlanta has very hot and humid summers, is mild during the fall and spring, and is cooler during the winter. In Casablanca, temperatures remain mild throughout the year. Provide at least one reason why these cities have such different climates even though they are at the same latitude.

8. Some hurricanes form near the coast of West Africa in the Atlantic Ocean, south of Casablanca. Atlanta is more likely to be affected by these hurricanes than Casablanca is. How do the movements of prevailing winds and ocean currents explain this difference?

9. How could meteorologists use this information to predict the path of a hurricane? Support your claim with evidence and reasoning.

Use the map to answer Questions 10–13.

Eria, an Imaginary Continent on Earth

Examine this map of an imaginary continent to explain weather and climate patterns.

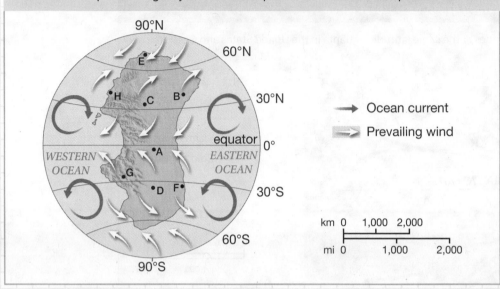

10. What factors are represented on this map that could potentially affect weather and climate on the continent?

11. Identify the location that you would most likely find a rain forest. Support your claim with evidence and reasoning.

12. The Eastern Ocean is warm between 0° and 30°S. What type of air mass likely forms here? How might this affect point A, which is at a low elevation?

13. Why might the climate in location H be different from the climate in location C?

Name: _____   Date: _____

What Influences Monsoon Season in the Southwestern United States?

Each year the Southwest region of the United States experiences monsoon season. Arizona and New Mexico receive half of their annual rainfall during this season. The monsoon season is a showcase of dramatic weather. While the storms suppress hot temperatures and revive vegetation, they also deliver intense rains, powerful winds, and a high number of lightning strikes. A number of factors influence the monsoon season.

You will collect evidence about how this weather pattern develops on a local, short-term basis, and then collect information about the longer-term patterns that exist. Why does it happen at a certain time of the year at this location? What factors influence the weather associated with a monsoon season? Do monsoon seasons change over time in this region? Are there other global patterns that can be predicted every year?

The steps below will help guide you in planning an investigation and constructing an explanation.

1. **Ask Questions** Develop a list of questions about monsoon seasons.

2. **Conduct Research** Find information about the monsoon season in the Southwest region of the United States. Describe what causes monsoons, what weather is associated with a monsoon, what global weather patterns influence the monsoon season there, when the season begins and ends, and patterns in past monsoon seasons in the Southwest.

3. **Analyze Data** Which local weather factors contribute to or influence how long the monsoon season lasts or how severe the weather is in the Southwest? What global weather patterns may influence the severity or longevity of the monsoon season?

4. **Interpret Data** Using the data from your research, what have you learned about past monsoon seasons in the Southwest? Have there been changes to monsoon seasons over time? Describe any historical data related to the monsoon season.

5. **Construct an Explanation** Explain local and global weather factors that contribute to a monsoon season and to any monsoon season changes. Provide evidence to support your claims.

✓ **Self-Check**

	I identified the local weather factors that influence the monsoon season in the Southwest region of the US.
	I researched both local and global weather factors that contribute to the characteristics of a monsoon season.
	I collected evidence about the history of monsoon seasons in the Southwest to determine if they change over time.
	I provided evidence to support my claim in regards to monsoon seasons changing over time.

Glossary

Pronunciation Key							
Sound	Symbol	Example	Respelling	Sound	Symbol	Example	Respelling
ă	a	pat	PAT	ŏ	ah	bottle	BAHT'l
ā	ay	pay	PAY	ō	oh	toe	TOH
âr	air	care	KAIR	ô	aw	caught	KAWT
ä	ah	father	FAH•ther	ôr	ohr	roar	ROHR
är	ar	argue	AR•gyoo	oi	oy	noisy	NOYZ•ee
ch	ch	chase	CHAYS	o͞o	u	book	BUK
ĕ	e	pet	PET	o͞o	oo	boot	BOOT
ĕ (at end of a syllable)	eh	settee lessee	seh•TEE leh•SEE	ou	ow	pound	POWND
ĕr	ehr	merry	MEHR•ee	s	s	center	SEN•ter
ē	ee	beach	BEECH	sh	sh	cache	CASH
g	g	gas	GAS	ŭ	uh	flood	FLUHD
ĭ	i	pit	PIT	ûr	er	bird	BERD
ĭ (at end of a syllable)	ih	guitar	gih•TAR	z	z	xylophone	ZY•luh•fohn
ī	y eye (only for a complete syllable)	pie island	PY EYE•luhnd	z	z	bags	BAGZ
îr	ir	hear	HIR	zh	zh	decision	dih•SIZH•uhn
j	j	germ	JERM	ə	uh	around broken focus	uh•ROWND BROH•kuhn FOH•kuhs
k	k	kick	KIK	ər	er	winner	WIN•er
ng	ng	thing	THING	th	th	thin they	THIN THAY
ngk	ngk	bank	BANGK	w	w	one	WUHN
				wh	hw	whether	HWETH•er

A–Z

air mass (AIR MAS)
    a large body of air throughout which temperature and moisture content are similar (87)
    masa de aire   un gran volumen de aire, cuya temperatura y cuyo contenido de humedad son similares en toda su extensión

climate (KLY•mit)
    the average weather conditions in an area over a long period of time (120)
    clima   las condiciones promedio del tiempo en un área durante un largo período de tiempo

condensation (kahn•den•SAY•shuhn)
    the change of state from a gas to a liquid (53)
    condensación   el cambio de estado de gas a líquido

convection (kuhn•VEK•shuhn)
    the movement of matter due to differences in density; the transfer of energy due to the movement of matter (9, 36)
    convección   el movimiento de la materia debido a diferencias en la densidad; la transferencia de energía debido al movimiento de la materia

Coriolis effect (kohr•ee•OH•lis ih•FEKT)
    the curving of the path of a moving object from an otherwise straight path due to Earth's rotation (12, 28)
    efecto de Coriolis   la desviación de la trayectoria recta que experimentan los objetos en movimiento debido a la rotación de la Tierra

deposition (dep·uh·ZISH·uhn)
    the change of state from a gas directly to a solid (54)
    sublimación inversa   cambio de estado por el cual un gas se convierte directamente en un sólido

evaporation (ee•vap•uh•RAY•shuhn)
    the change of state from a liquid to a gas that usually occurs at the surface of a liquid over a wide range of temperatures (52)
    evaporación   el cambio de estado de líquido a gaseoso que ocurre generalmente en la superficie de un líquido en un amplio rango de temperaturas

front (FRUHNT)
    the boundary between air masses of different densities and usually different temperatures (89)
    frente   el límite entre masas de aire de diferentes densidades y, normalmente, diferentes temperaturas

ocean current (OH•shuhn KER•uhnt)
    a movement of ocean water that follows a regular pattern (26)
    corriente oceánica   un movimiento del agua del océano que sigue un patrón regular

precipitation (prih•sip•ih•TAY•shuhn)
    any form of water that falls to Earth's surface from the clouds (54)
    precipitación   cualquier forma de agua que cae de las nubes a la superficie de la Tierra

runoff (RUHN•awf)
    precipitation that flows over the land and into streams and rivers (56)
    escurrimiento   precipitación que fluye sobre la tierra y llega a los arroyos y a los ríos

sublimation (suhb•luh•MAY•shuhn)
    the change of state from a solid directly to a gas (52)
    sublimación   cambio de estado por el cual un sólido se convierte directamente en un gas

transpiration (tran•spuh•RAY•shuhn)
    the process by which plants release water vapor into the air through a leaf or stem (52)
    transpiración   proceso por el cual las plantas liberan vapor de agua al aire a través de una hoja o un tallo

water cycle (WAW•ter SY•kuhl)
    the continuous movement of water between the atmosphere, the land, the oceans, and living things (59)
    ciclo del agua   el movimiento continuo del agua entre la atmósfera, la tierra, los océanos y los seres vivos

weather (WETH•er)
    the short-term state of the atmosphere, including temperature, humidity, precipitation, wind, and visibility (80)
    tiempo   el estado de la atmósfera a corto plazo que incluye la temperatura, la humedad, la precipitación, el viento y la visibilidad

weather forecast (WETH•er FOHR•kast)
    a prediction about the state of the atmosphere for a given location and time (108)
    pronóstico del tiempo   predicción acerca del estado de la atmósfera en un lugar y un momento determinados

Index

Note: Italic page numbers represent illustrative material, such as figures, tables, margin elements, photographs, and illustrations. Boldface page numbers represent page numbers for definitions.

H

hail, 54, *54*
Hands-On Lab
 Explore Density Differences in
  Water, 31–32
 Model an Air Mass Interaction, 88
 Model the Formation of Clouds and
  Rain, 53
 Model the Formation of Wind, 7-8
 Model Your Climate, 131
 Predict Costs Using a Model,
  105–106
heating/cooling system, 9
hemispheres, 14, *14*
high-pressure bands, 12, *12*
high-pressure belts, 126, *126*
high-pressure system, 85, *85*
horse latitudes, 13, *13*, 22, *22*
hot air balloon, 6, *6*
**humans, percentage of water in the
  body,** 47
humidity
 as aspect of climate, 121
 effect on snowflakes, *95–96*
 as element of weather, 80
 in weather forecasts, 108, *109*
humid tropical climate, 132, *132*
hurricane, 16, 75, *75*
hydrologist, 63–64, *63*
hydrosphere, 36, 91

I

ice
 on Earth's surface, 55, *58*
 water of, 47, 48, 49
iceberg, 58
ice caps, 58
ice climbing, *120, 139*
ice crystals in atmosphere, 53
infiltration, 56, *57*
influences of weather
 describing weather, 80–83
 explaining how fronts change
  weather, 87–90

 identifying weather associated with
  pressure systems, 84–86
 relating earth system interactions to
  weather, 91–96
interaction
 between Earth's systems, 36
 between Earth's systems and
  weather, 91–96
Interactive Review, 23, 45, 67, 99,
  117, 139
Interpret a Weather Map, 86
interpret data, 146
investigation process
 analyze data, 74, 146
 ask a question, 73
 communicate, 74
 conduct research, 74, 146
 construct explanation, 146
 identify and recommend
  solution, 74
 interpret data, 146
isobar, 84, *84, 85*

J

jet streams, 19–20, *19*

K

kinetic energy, 18
kiteboarding, *1*

L

Lake City, Colorado, *120*
land, water movement on, 55–58, *55*
landforms
 effect on climate, 126, 128
 effect on weather, 93–94
Language SmArts, 11, 37, 62, 112, 131
 Compare and Contrast
  Information, 90
 Describe Weather, 83
latitude, 122, **122**
 effect on weather, *143*
 identifying, *77*

lava lamp, 9
Lesson Self-Check, 21–23, 43–45,
  65–67, 97–99, 115–117, 137–139
Life Science Connection
 Crocodile Surfers! 68
 Sleep Flying? 68
**limitations on weather
  prediction,** 111, *111*
lines of latitude, 14
liquid, water as, 49, *50*
low-pressure bands, 12, *12*
low-pressure belts, 126, *126*
low-pressure system, 85, *85*

M

map, weather, *84,* 86, *86,* 89, *98, 101,
  102, 110, 115, 117, 141*
marine organisms, 39, *39*
mathematical models, 103
 limitations of, 104
 making predictions with,
  102–107, 117
 for weather forecasting, 109, 111
matter
 cycling in atmosphere, 15–16, *15,
  23, 23*
 cycling of, *45,* 61
 flow of in ocean water, 36–40, *39, 40*
mechanical energy, 18
Mediterranean Sea, 35, *35*
melting, 49–50, *50,* 55, 59
meteorologist, 113–114, *113*
methane, as greenhouse gas,
  135–136, *136*
migration, 102
millibar (mb), 82, 84
mist, 53
models/modeling
 air mass interaction, 88
 climate graphs, 121, *121*
 cost prediction, 105–106
 of Earth's atmosphere, 53
 of Earth's rotation, 11, *11*
 evaluating of, 3
 of global winds, 13, *13*
 making predictions with, 102–107,
  102, 102, 117, *117*

mathematical models, 102–107, 103, 104, 109, 111, 117
of process, 103, *103*, 117, *117*
of rain, 3
of regional climates, 130–134, *130*
surface currents, 26–29, *27*
of water cycle, 56, 59–62, *60*, 67
for weather forecasting, 109, 111, *117*, 121
wind and convection, 6
of your climate, 131
monsoon, 145–146, *145*
Moscow, Russia, 133, *133*
mountain range
effect on climate, 118, 128, *128*
effect on weather, 93–94, *94*
movement
air pressure, 87
atmosphere, 51–54, *52*, 56
cloud, 17, *17*
of glaciers, 58, *58*
water in Earth's atmosphere, 51–54
water in Earth's surface, 55–58
multimedia presentation, 131

N

nautilus, *102*
New Mexico, 145
nitrogen cycle, 16
nitrogen in atmosphere, 51
nitrous oxide, as greenhouse gas, 135–136
North Atlantic Drift, 92
Northern Hemisphere, 14, *14*, 19
North Pole, 12, 13, *13*, 14, *14*, 122–123, *123*, *126*

O

occluded front, 89, *89*, 90
ocean
circulation of, 24–45, *24*, 55–56, *55*
deep ocean currents, 30–35, *34*, *35*, 45, 55–56, *55*
density differences in, 30–33
effect on climate, 127, 128

effect on weather, 91, 92–93, 113
evaporation from, 52
global circulation, 38–40, *38*, *40*
in Mediterranean Sea, 35, *35*
surface currents, 127
water of, 47, 48
waves of, 18
ocean current, 24–45, *24*, **26,** *60*
deep, 30–35, *34*, *35*, 45, 55–56, *55*, 127
effect of wind on, 18, 127
effect on weather, 91
effect on winds, 92, *93*
factors affecting deep currents, 34
flow of matter and energy in, 36–40, *40*
global ocean circulation, 38–40, *38*, *40*
surface, 18, 26–29, *27*, *29*, 127
online activities, Explore ONLINE!
9, 26, 30, 57, 79, 94, 97, 101, 115, 126
organic material, cycling in atmosphere, 16
organisms, needs of, 47
oxygen
in atmosphere, 51
in ocean water, 39
ozone, as greenhouse gases, 135–136, *136*

P

particles, in atmosphere, 6
patterns
global wind, 13, *13*, 28, 92, *94*, 127
in the ocean, 26–35, *27*, *28*, *29*, *34*, *35*, *37*, *38*
of precipitation, 94, *94*, 113–114
of prevailing winds, 92, *92*, 93, *93*, 98
of rainfall, 113, 114
of snowflake formation, 95–96, *95*, *96*
People in Science, 113–114
Phoenix, Arizona, 129, *129*
phosphorus, 5, 16, 21

photosynthesis, 16, 39, 40, *40*
physical oceanographer, 41–42, *41*
Physical Science Connection
High Altitude Weather Balloons, 140
plankton, 39, *39*
plants
role in carbon cycle, 16
transpiration of, 52
use of nitrogen, 16
polar climate, 133, *133*
polar easterlies, 13, *13*
polar jet stream, *19*
poles, 122–123, *123*, *126*
pollution, 16, 39, 61
precipitation, **54,** *60*, 81
as aspect of climate, 120, 121
in deserts, 119
effect on ocean salinity, 33
factors affecting, 113, 126
in Flagstaff and Phoenix, 129, *129*
formation of, 90
ocean currents' effect on, 55
probability of, *112*
in rain forests, 119
in San Francisco, California, 120, *120*
in water cycle, *46*, 53–54
in weather forecasts, 108, *109*
prediction
about climate, *117*, 121
of air temperature, 107
of change in ocean circulation, 40, *40*
effects of change in ocean circulation, 40
of floating or sinking, 31, *31*
with mathematical models, 102–107
mathematical models limits of, 111, *111*
models for making, 102–107, 117, *117*
of weather, 88, 100–117, *100*, *111*
weather patterns, 108–112
of wind direction, 10
pressure system, *85*
prevailing winds and, 92
weather, 85–86